More Praise for

QUEER AS ALL GET OUT

"An outstanding collection of the vital stories of important and under-heralded queer figures, paired with Shelby Criswell's excellent art and a touching personal narrative."

—MATT LUBCHANSKY, artist and associate editor of *The Nib*

"An illuminating read about the lives of ten lesser-known queer historical heroes, drawn in an engaging and personable fashion."

—MELANIE GILLMAN, author of *As the Crow Flies* and *Stage Dreams*

"An exciting, essential addition to the queer canon. Shining a light on a diverse group on extraordinary queer folks from the past, and reminding us exactly why these stories are so vital. This book is a treasure!"

—ASHLEY ROBIN FRANKLIN, author of *That Full Moon Feeling*

"Books like this are so important! Just by reading about the queer activists of our past, a community forms around you. And that community will give you power."

—STEENZ, cartoonist of *Heart of the City*

"A heartfelt love letter to the oft-forgot pioneers of the global queer movement."

—RONNIE GARCIA, illustrator in *Puerto Rico Strong*

SHELBY CRISWELL

QUEER AS ALL GET OUT

10 PEOPLE WHO'VE INSPIRED ME

STREET NOISE

Street Noise Books • Brooklyn, New York

ISBN 978-1951-491-07-9

Edited by Katie Fricas
Book design by Liz Frances

Printed in South Korea

9 8 7 6 5 4 3 2

First Edition

TABLE OF CONTENTS

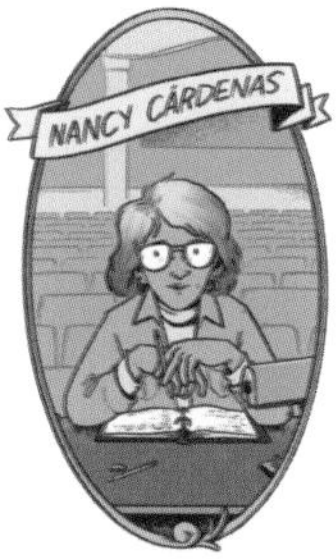
NANCY CÁRDENAS

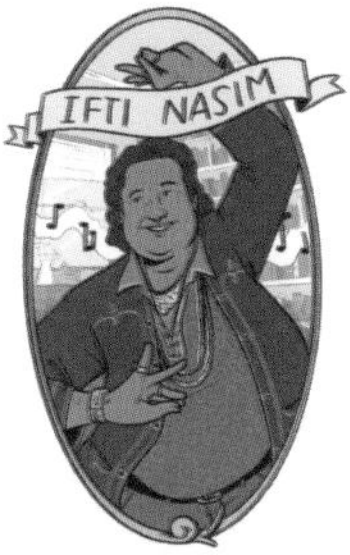
IFTI NASIM

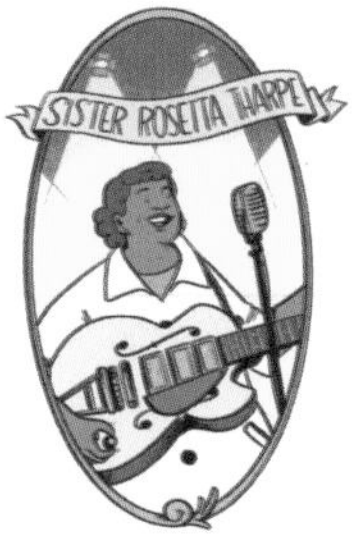
SISTER ROSETTA THARPE

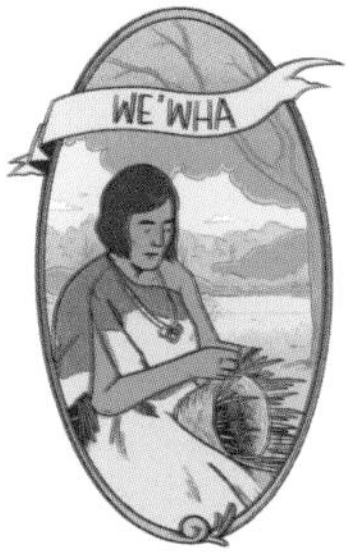
WE'WHA

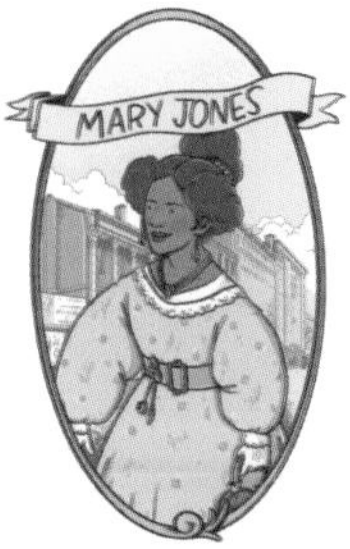
MARY JONES

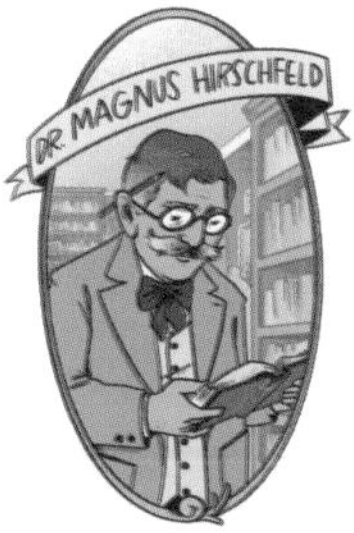
DR MAGNUS HIRSCHFELD

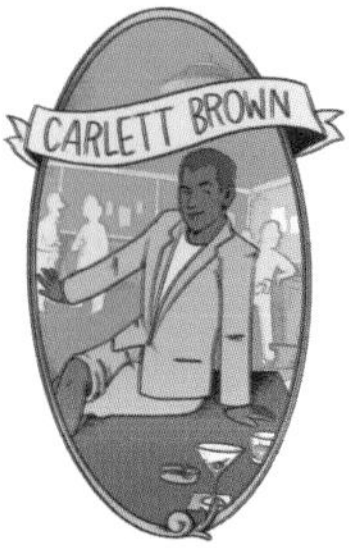
CARLETT BROWN

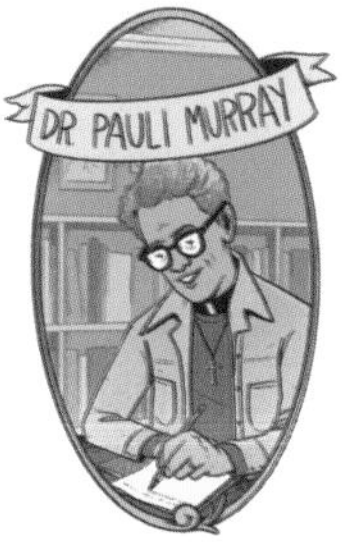
DR PAULI MURRAY

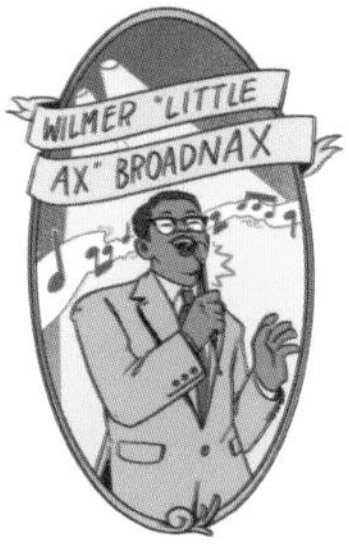
WILMER "LITTLE
AX" BROADNAX

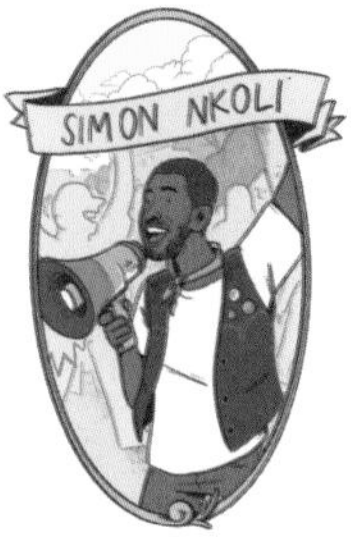
SIMON NKOLI

PHOTO BY PHILIP BARR

Living with AIDS

The days of his life became more precious to Doug Pearce, 22, after he was diagnosed as having AIDS. See story on
Page 9 A

FOR UNCLE DOUG.

I NEVER GOT TO MEET YOU,
BUT I THINK ABOUT YOU OFTEN.

IN THE SWELTERING HEAT OF SAN ANTONIO, TEXAS ...

SAN ANTO COFFEE ROASTERS

Hi, I'll get a- uhh, Americano and a concha.

That'll be $5.10, friend.

SITUATIONS LIKE THIS ONE, WHERE MY GENDER ISN'T IMMEDIATELY ASSUMED, DON'T HAPPEN THAT OFTEN.

Thanks!

NORMALLY, I GET CALLED "MA'AM" OR "SIR."

SOMETIMES I GET THE "SIR -ER UHH SORRY, MA'AM" MISHAP, WHERE THE CASHIER CANNOT DECIPHER MY GENDER UNTIL THEY HEAR THE PITCH OF MY VOICE.

IT DOESN'T BOTHER ME THAT MUCH. I KINDA LIKE MY GENDER BEING MYSTERIOUS. IT'S A HELL OF A LOT BETTER THAN TRYING TO EXPLAIN THE CONCEPT OF THE GENDER BINARY TO A COMPLETE STRANGER.

THE AMERICAN SOUTH CAN BE A SCARY PLACE TO LIVE AT TIMES. MY CITY, SAN ANTONIO, IS SOMEWHAT PROGRESSIVE, SO IT DOESN'T SEEM AS THREATENING AS MORE CONSERVATIVE SOUTHERN TOWNS.

BUT LIVING HERE, I DO GET UNWANTED ATTENTION FOR BEING VISIBLY QUEER. I'M SUSCEPTIBLE TO ALL KINDS OF WEIRD GLANCES, NAME-CALLING, AND OTHER FORMS OF BIGOTRY.

THE WAY I LOOK OR AM DOESN'T MEAN I DESERVE HATRED. SAME GOES FOR ALL OF MY FELLOW QUEER AND TRANSGENDER FRIENDS. NONE OF US **EVER** DESERVES TO BE GAWKED AT LIKE CIRCUS ANIMALS.

I'VE ALWAYS LIVED IN THE AMERICAN SOUTH, OR "THE BIBLE BELT."

SOUTHERN PRIDE IS TRICKY FOR ME. I LOVE TEXAS, BUT I ALSO FEEL THIS REGION'S RELIGIOUS AND TRADITIONAL VALUES CREATE INJUSTICE.

I HAVE QUEER FRIENDS WHO WERE KICKED OUT OF THEIR FAMILIES' HOMES AT A YOUNG AGE FOR "GOING AGAINST THE BIBLE."

A LOT OF PEOPLE I KNOW STRUGGLE WITH THIS INTERNAL TUG OF WAR: BEING PROUD AND ASHAMED OF HOME AT THE SAME TIME.

MY PRIDE COMES FROM POSITIVE THINGS I'VE FOUND HERE, LIKE MY CHOSEN FAMILY AND COMMUNITY.

PLUS, SOUTHERN FOOD IS DELECTABLY GREASY AND DELICIOUS!

I GREW UP IN A FAMILY OF SOUTHERN BAPTISTS. MY GREAT AUNT AND GREAT GRANDPA WERE MINISTERS. WE ALL HAD A HAND IN RUNNING THE CHURCH.

I ONLY RECENTLY LEARNED THAT THE SOUTHERN BAPTIST CONVENTION SUPPORTED SLAVERY AND SPLIT FROM THE NORTHERN BAPTIST CONVENTION OVER THE ISSUE.

THE NORTHERN BAPTIST CONVENTION BELIEVED IN ABOLITION OF SLAVERY, SO FOUR SLAVE-OWNING MEMBERS LEFT AND STARTED THE SOUTHERN BAPTIST CONVENTION IN 1845.

THE SOUTHERN BAPTIST CONVENTION DIDN'T APOLOGIZE FOR ITS SUPPORT OF SLAVERY AND SEGREGATION UNTIL 1995.

THE SERMONS, TO ME, ALWAYS SEEMED TO WARP THE BIBLE TO FIT CERTAIN TRADITIONALIST AGENDAS. AT THE TIME, I DIDN'T KNOW THAT MY BAPTIST FAITH WAS BUILT ON RACISM.

RELIGION HELPED ME MAKE PEACE WITH MY FATHER'S DEATH FROM COLON CANCER AND MADE ME FEEL IMPORTANT AND LOVED DURING MY MOTHER'S ADDICTION ISSUES, BUT CHURCH MEMBERS STILL QUOTED ANTI-GAY BIBLE VERSES AT ME.

I WAS TOLD MY SEXUALITY WAS A SIN AND AN ABOMINATION.

TO COPE, I SOMETIMES PLACED MYSELF BACK IN THE CLOSET.

I WENT TO CHURCH WITH MY FAMILY, BUT I DIDN'T REALLY BELIEVE IN GOD ANYMORE.

SOMETIMES, IT FELT LIKE I WOULD NEVER ESCAPE THIS DROWNING FEELING. THE HURT WILL NEVER FULLY GO AWAY.

IN SECOND GRADE, I KNEW THAT I WAS QUEER.

Hello students, I want everyone to put down their pencils for a minute. We have a new student joining our class!

Everyone, this is Carly. She will be in our class for the rest of the year, so make her feel welcome.

February 24, 2002

Agenda:

1.
2.
3.

WHEN MY FIRST CRUSH WAS A GIRL, I KNEW.

I NEVER TOLD ANYONE I LIKED CARLY, AND I NEVER LET IT BOTHER ME THAT I LIKED A GIRL. I WAS ALSO IN THE SECOND GRADE! ROMANTIC ENDEAVORS TOOK A BACK SEAT TO PICKING MY NOSE AND PLAYING VIDEO GAMES.

IN MIDDLE SCHOOL, MY CLOSE FRIENDS KNEW I WAS QUEER, EVEN THOUGH I HADN'T FORMALLY COME OUT TO EVERYONE YET.

IN HIGH SCHOOL, I FIT THE MOVIE AND TV SHOW STEREOTYPE OF A QUEER TEENAGER.

I WAS 1st LIEUTENANT OF THE COLORGUARD TEAM, ART CLUB PRESIDENT, AND INVOLVED IN THEATRE. I MIGHT AS WELL HAVE BEEN A CHARACTER IN THE TV SHOW, *GLEE*.

I HAD PRIDE, EVEN WHEN KIDS AT SCHOOL WERE NASTY TO ME, BUT MY ONLINE FRIENDS GAVE ME THE CONFIDENCE TO LIVE KINDLY AND AUTHENTICALLY, SOMETHING I'M STILL GRATEFUL FOR TO THIS DAY.

Faggot.

I THOUGHT HIGH SCHOOL WAS STUPID. I'D TELL MYSELF, "JUST GET IT OVER WITH AND THEN YOU'LL BE ABLE TO TRULY LIVE YOUR LIFE."

Have a nice day!

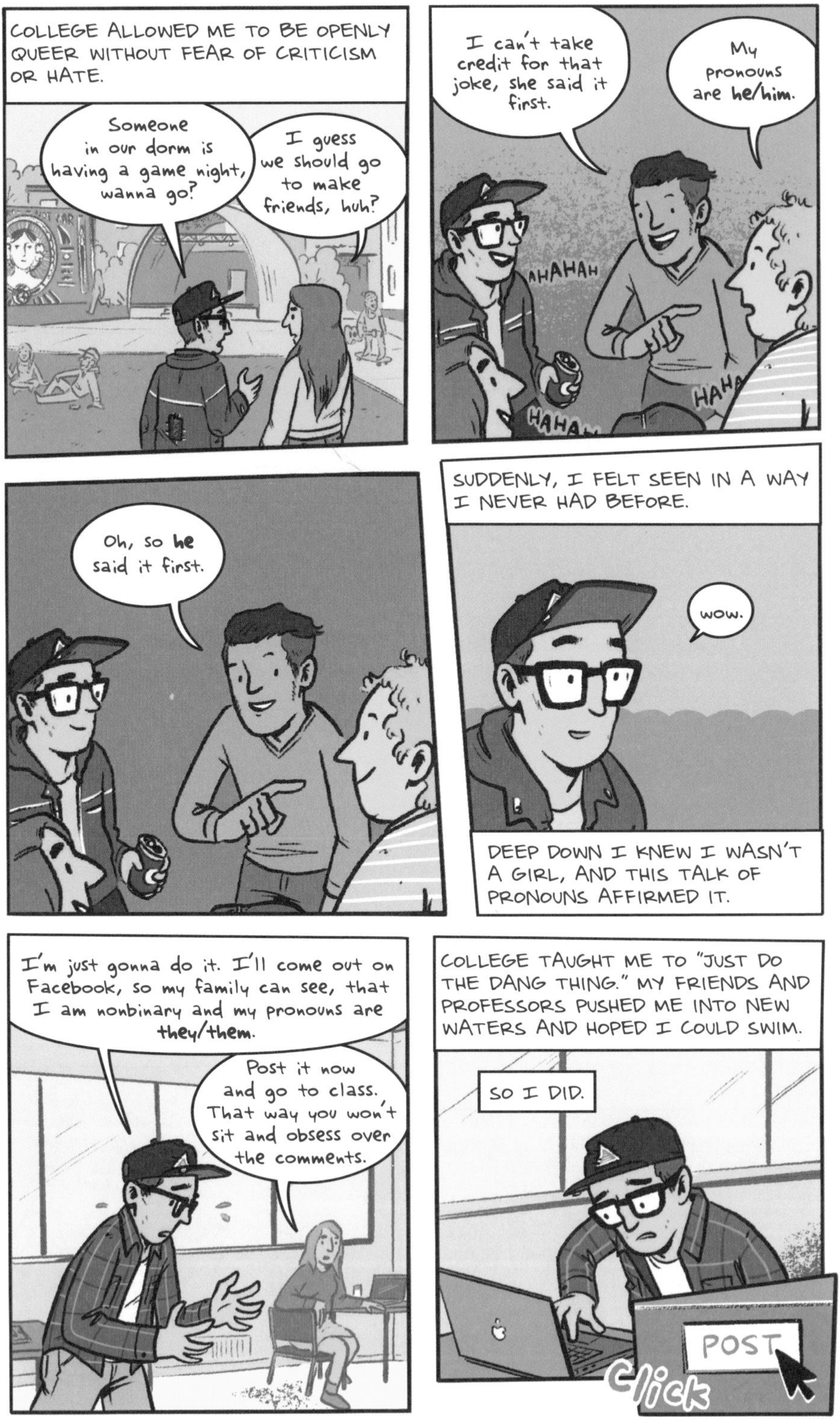
COLLEGE ALLOWED ME TO BE OPENLY QUEER WITHOUT FEAR OF CRITICISM OR HATE.
Someone in our dorm is having a game night, wanna go?
I guess we should go to make friends, huh?
I can't take credit for that joke, she said it first.
My pronouns are **he/him**.
AHAHAH
HAHAH
HAHA
Oh, so **he** said it first.
SUDDENLY, I FELT SEEN IN A WAY I NEVER HAD BEFORE.
WOW.
DEEP DOWN I KNEW I WASN'T A GIRL, AND THIS TALK OF PRONOUNS AFFIRMED IT.
I'm just gonna do it. I'll come out on Facebook, so my family can see, that I am nonbinary and my pronouns are **they/them**.
Post it now and go to class. That way you won't sit and obsess over the comments.
COLLEGE TAUGHT ME TO "JUST DO THE DANG THING." MY FRIENDS AND PROFESSORS PUSHED ME INTO NEW WATERS AND HOPED I COULD SWIM.
SO I DID.
POST
Click

MY FRIENDS AND I WENT TO A TRANSGENDER SUPPORT GROUP A FEW TIMES. IT WAS COOL TO SEE AND INTERACT WITH TRANS PEOPLE WHO WERE OLDER THAN US.

Can you recall a moment in your life that set in motion the journey for you to recognize that you are transgender?

THOSE MOMENTS FOR ME WERE COLLEGE AND SECOND GRADE.

I WAS SO YOUNG.

That group made me realize everyone figures out their gender at a different pace. Thankfully, the language of gender and sexuality continues to expand. There are more resources now than there were a few decades ago when my aunt and uncle came out as queer to my family.

If you're in need of help or info pertaining to your gender and/or sexuality, check the References and Further Reading sections in the back of the book!

ONE OF MY TRANSGENDER SUPPORT GROUP MEMBERS MENTIONED FINDING SOLACE IN NANCY CARDENA'S STORY.

THEY, LIKE NANCY, HAD NOT FULLY COME OUT UNTIL LATER IN LIFE.

I WAS SO YOUNG WHEN I FIGURED OUT MY GENDER IDENTITY AND SEXUALITY. HOW DIFFERENT WOULD MY LIFE BE IF I HAD WAITED UNTIL I WAS OLDER TO COME OUT?

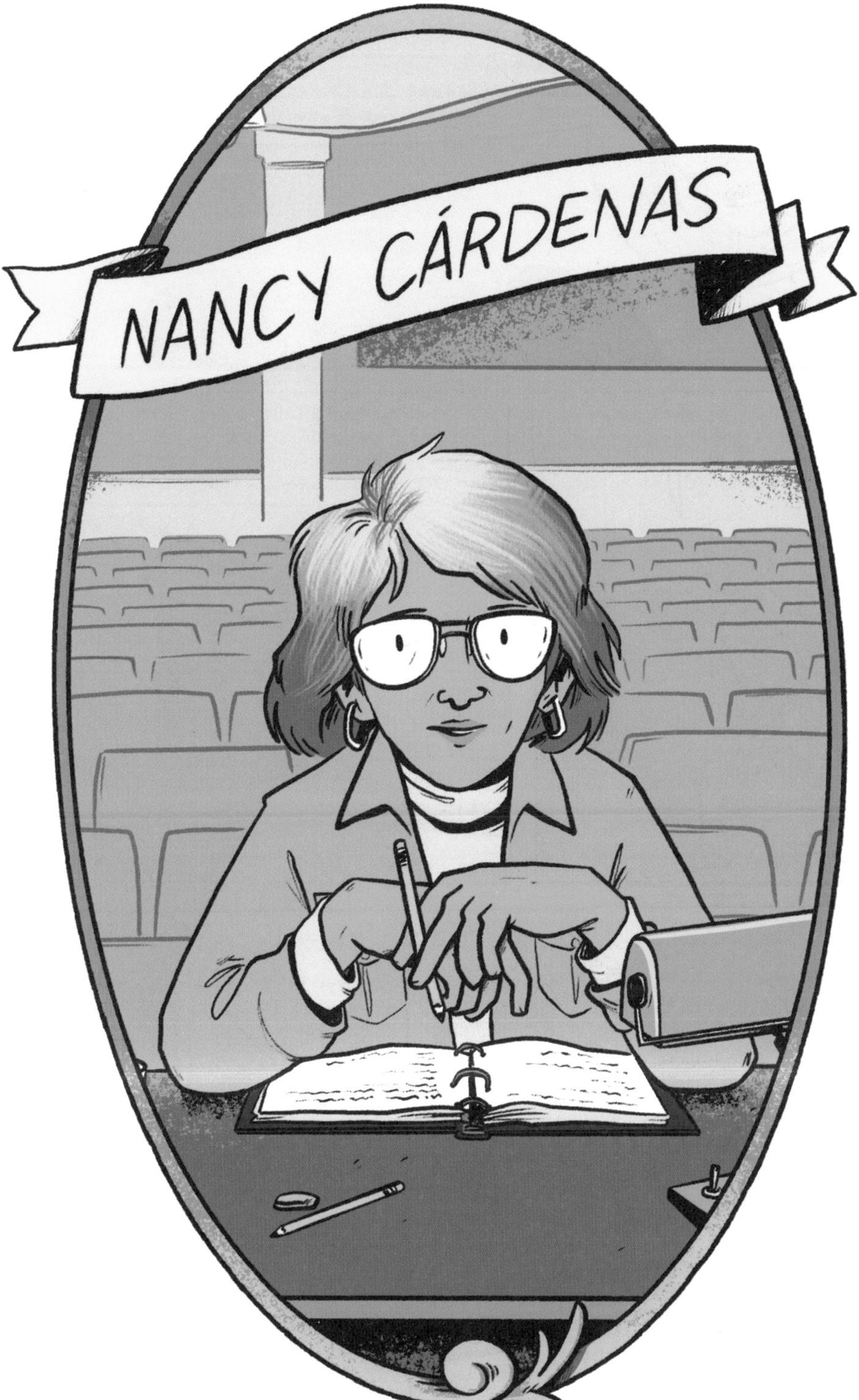
NANCY CÁRDENAS

CUT!

Remember, I'd like this scene to have some humor to it. Make the audience laugh.

Reflect on that, okay? Let's break for lunch.

NANCY CÁRDENAS DIDN'T COME OUT UNTIL HER LATE 30s, DURING A TIME IN MEXICO WHEN QUEER PEOPLE WERE OFTEN MENTALLY TORTURED AND SHUNNED FOR THEIR IDENTITIES.

Ah, Nancy!

¿La usual? ¿Torta de aguacate?

Sí, y extra cilantro, por favor.

*Ah, Nancy! The usual? Avocado Torta?

12

*Yes, and extra cilantro, please.

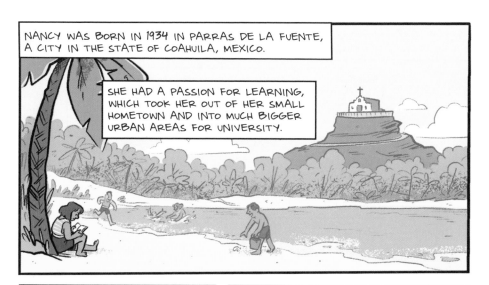

NANCY WAS BORN IN 1934 IN PARRAS DE LA FUENTE, A CITY IN THE STATE OF COAHUILA, MEXICO.

SHE HAD A PASSION FOR LEARNING, WHICH TOOK HER OUT OF HER SMALL HOMETOWN AND INTO MUCH BIGGER URBAN AREAS FOR UNIVERSITY.

URBAN LIFE IN PLACES LIKE MEXICO CITY ALLOWED NANCY TO DEVELOP A LONG LIST OF INTERESTS.

BECAUSE NANCY SPENT SO MANY YEARS IN SCHOOL, HER FAMILY HOPED SHE'D BECOME A DOCTOR OR A LAWYER...

BUT NO!

HER UNIVERSITY STUDIES IN FILM, THEATRE, LANGUAGE, AND LITERATURE MADE HER FALL IN LOVE WITH THE POWER OF WORDS.

WHILE AT UNIVERSITY IN MEXICO CITY, NANCY AND HER FRIENDS CAMPAIGNED FOR THE COMMUNIST PARTY.

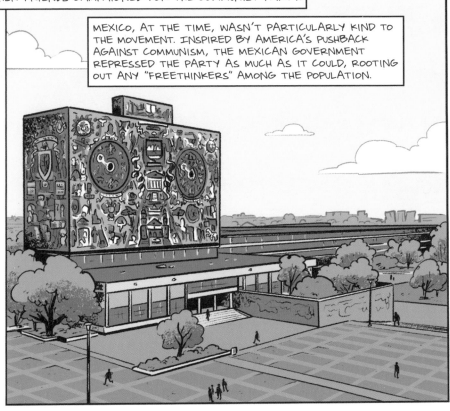

MEXICO, AT THE TIME, WASN'T PARTICULARLY KIND TO THE MOVEMENT. INSPIRED BY AMERICA'S PUSHBACK AGAINST COMMUNISM, THE MEXICAN GOVERNMENT REPRESSED THE PARTY AS MUCH AS IT COULD, ROOTING OUT ANY "FREETHINKERS" AMONG THE POPULATION.

BUT NANCY REMAINED PASSIONATE, FREELY SPEAKING AT RALLIES AND HANDING OUT PAMPHLETS THAT SHE HAD WRITTEN.

HER WELL-CRAFTED WRITING CONVINCED QUITE A FEW PEOPLE TO BECOME MEMBERS OF THE COMMUNIST PARTY.

TAP!

FOR THE FIRST TIME, SHE WAS SEEN NOT ONLY AS AN ACTIVIST, BUT AS A **WRITER**.

Thank you for this! You've changed a lot of my outlook on life.

AFTER UNIVERSITY, SHE JOINED AN ALLIANCE OF ARTISTS, WRITERS, AND INTELLECTUALS. THEY WROTE ARTICLES AGAINST AUTHORITARIANISM AND FOR DEMOCRATIC REFORM WITHIN MEXICO.

Yeah, this is good.

NANCY'S LOVE OF WRITING DIDN'T STOP AT HER ACTIVIST WORK. SHE BEGAN TO WRITE HER OWN PLAYS AND WORKED AS A TRANSLATOR.

Want to take a break from reading lines?

THE ACTIVIST COMMUNITY TAUGHT NANCY ABOUT QUEER SUBCULTURES.

"Homosexual Radical Change Now"...

Vaya, esto es de America.

NANCY EXPLORED THAT SUBCULTURE AS SHE AND HER FRIENDS DRESSED IN MASCULINE GARB. AT THE TIME, UNISEX CLOTHING WAS NOT COMMONPLACE. THEIR LOOKS SUBVERTED NORMS ABOUT HOW A WOMAN SHOULD LOOK.

Tu tio tiene bien sabor. ¡Gracias!

*Wow, this is from America.

*Your uncle has good taste. Thank you!

NANCY'S ACTIVISM, EDITORIAL WORK, AND PLAYS GAINED HER REGIONAL RECOGNITION. PEOPLE BEGAN TO KNOW HER NAME.

Hola, Nancy.

SHE EXPANDED HER INFLUENCE BY APPEARING ON NUMEROUS RADIO AND TELEVISION SHOWS. IN 1973, SHE WAS A GUEST ON MEXICO'S MOST WATCHED NEWS PROGRAM, *24 HORAS*.

24 HORAS

Jacob! Hola.

Oh, Nancy! Bienvenidos.

WHEN WORD GOT OUT ABOUT A STORE FIRING ONE OF ITS EMPLOYEES FOR BEING GAY, NANCY WAS INVITED ONTO THE SHOW TO DISCUSS QUEER RIGHTS.

*Jacob! Hello.   *Oh, Nancy! Welcome.

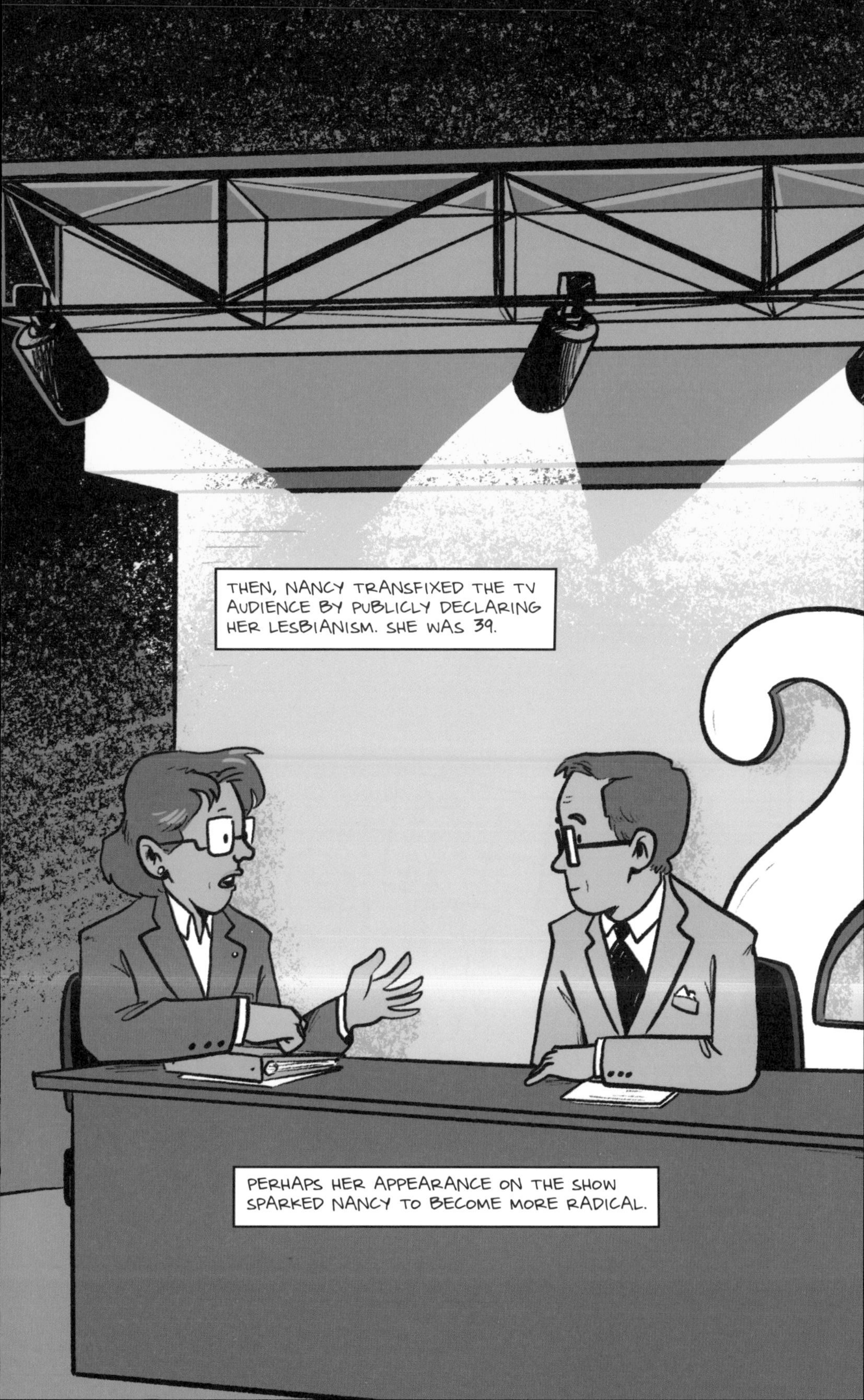
THEN, NANCY TRANSFIXED THE TV AUDIENCE BY PUBLICLY DECLARING HER LESBIANISM. SHE WAS 39.
PERHAPS HER APPEARANCE ON THE SHOW SPARKED NANCY TO BECOME MORE RADICAL.

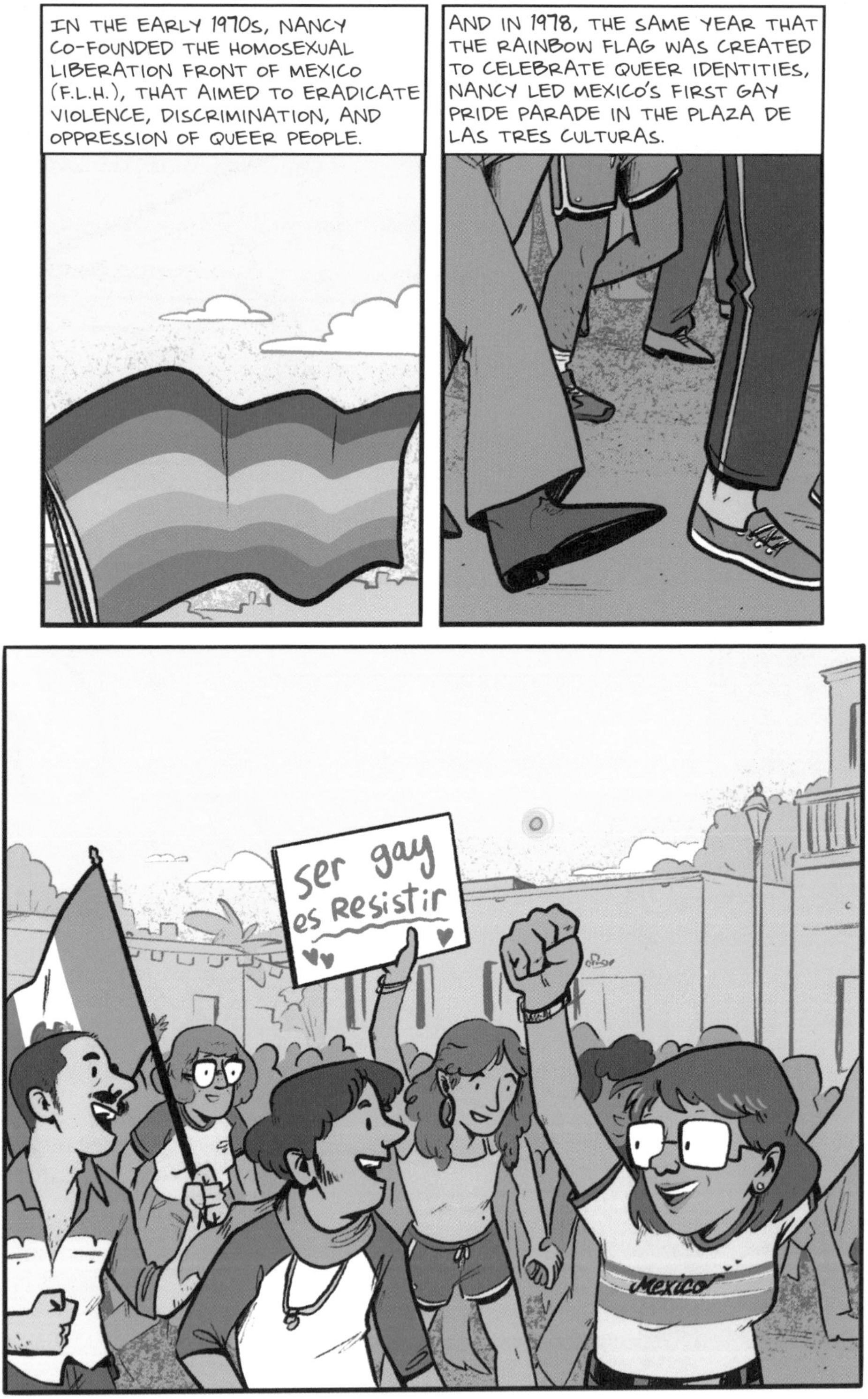
IN THE EARLY 1970s, NANCY CO-FOUNDED THE HOMOSEXUAL LIBERATION FRONT OF MEXICO (F.L.H.), THAT AIMED TO ERADICATE VIOLENCE, DISCRIMINATION, AND OPPRESSION OF QUEER PEOPLE.
AND IN 1978, THE SAME YEAR THAT THE RAINBOW FLAG WAS CREATED TO CELEBRATE QUEER IDENTITIES, NANCY LED MEXICO'S FIRST GAY PRIDE PARADE IN THE PLAZA DE LAS TRES CULTURAS.
ser gay es Resistir
Mexico

NANCY NEVER QUIT ACTIVISM.

SHE CONTINUED TO COMPOSE MANIFESTOS, GATHERED WITH OTHER QUEER WRITERS, ATTENDED LESBIAN CONFERENCES IN LATIN AMERICA AND THE CARIBBEAN, AND BECAME INVOLVED IN HER LOCAL THEATRE SCENE.

HER SCRIPTS WERE OVERTLY LESBIAN AND QUEER IN NATURE, SPEAKING TO A NEED TO UTILIZE HER PUBLIC "OUT" STATUS TO INCREASE THE VISIBILITY AND REPRESENTATION OF LATINX LESBIANS AND QUEER PEOPLE.

NANCY WANTED HER PLAYS TO BE RELATABLE ENOUGH TO COMPEL QUEER AUDIENCES, AND THE GENERAL PUBLIC AS WELL.

Okay, ladies, back to your positions!

Like I said earlier, I want this act to reach everyone. Think back on how awkward it was to be young and in love, channel that feeling.

Now, act two from the top!

SHE SPENT THE REST OF HER LIFE IN THEATRE. THE TRANSLATION SKILLS SHE ACQUIRED IN UNIVERSITY WERE HANDY IN CONVERTING LESBIAN PLAYS AND OTHER QUEER-WRITTEN WORKS INTO BOTH SPANISH AND POLISH.

IN 1992, SHE FOUNDED SER HUMANA, AN ORGANIZATION THAT BENEFITED ADULTS AND CHILDREN LIVING WITH AIDS.

LUCKILY, HER ELITE STATUS IN THE LOCAL THEATRE SCENE GAVE HER AN "IN" WITH CELEBRITIES, WHICH HELPED DRIVE SPONSORSHIPS AND DONATIONS TOWARD THE ORGANIZATION.

WHILE NANCY HAD BEEN FIGHTING FOR THOSE SICK WITH AIDS, SHE HAD BEEN BATTLING HER OWN ILLNESS, BREAST CANCER, WHICH SADLY TOOK HER LIFE IN 1994.

IN THE YEAR AFTER HER DEATH, A LESBIAN HISTORY ARCHIVE WAS ERECTED IN MEXICO CITY TO HONOR HER, EL CENTRO DE DOCUMENTACION Y ARCHIVO HISTORICO DE MEXICO, AMERICA Y EL CARIBE NANCY CÁRDENAS (C.D.A.H.L.).

*The Nancy Cárdenas Latin America and Mexican Lesbian Documentation and Historical Archives Center

NANCY'S WORKS NEVER RECEIVED MUCH INTERNATIONAL RECOGNITION, BUT RECENTLY SOME LGBTQ+ AND LATINX COMMUNITIES IN AMERICA AND MEXICO HAVE SPOTLIGHTED HER NAME WHEN TALKING ABOUT MEXICAN QUEER HISTORY AND THE ROLE SHE PLAYED AS A CHAMPION FOR GAY RIGHTS.

HONRAMOS A NUESTROS ANTEPASADOS

PRIDE

LA HOMOPHOBIA ESTÁ OUT!

NANCY INSPIRES ME TO BE COURAGEOUS. HER LIFE IS A REMINDER THAT IT IS NEVER TOO LATE TO COME OUT, AND HER ACTIVISM SERVES AS A TESTAMENT THAT CHANGE IS NECESSARY TO ERADICATE INJUSTICE.

NANCY, AND OTHER QUEER CREATORS, MAKE ME THANKFUL FOR THE SUBTLE AND OVERTLY GAY SUBJECT MATTER I SAW IN MOVIES, BOOKS, AND ON THE INTERNET WHEN I WAS YOUNGER.

AS A KID, I REMEMBER MY MOM WATCHED *WILL & GRACE*. THE TWO MAIN MALE CHARACTERS WERE GAY, AND ONE OF THE SIDE CHARACTERS WAS BISEXUAL.

I BELIEVE THAT SHOW MIGHT HAVE BEEN THE FIRST PIECE OF QUEER MEDIA I CONSUMED AS A CHILD.

QUEER AND TRANS REPRESENTATION IN MEDIA IS VITAL BECAUSE IT CAN HELP PEOPLE REALIZE THAT THEY AREN'T ALONE IN THEIR STRUGGLES.

I've identified the life form known as "gaylien."

PORTRAYING **LGBTQ+** LIVES POSITIVELY CAN HELP THOSE OUTSIDE THE COMMUNITY SEE THAT WE AREN'T VILLAINS OR MENACES TO SOCIETY.

I REMEMBER A DISCUSSION I ONCE HAD WITH A FRIEND ON GAY POETS.

Dude, I only know queer American poets!

Okay! Welcome to Non-American Queer Poets 101.

I recommend you first read Ifti Nasim's work. He was a gay poet from Pakistan.

He fled Pakistan to escape sexual persecution and avoid an arranged hetero marriage.

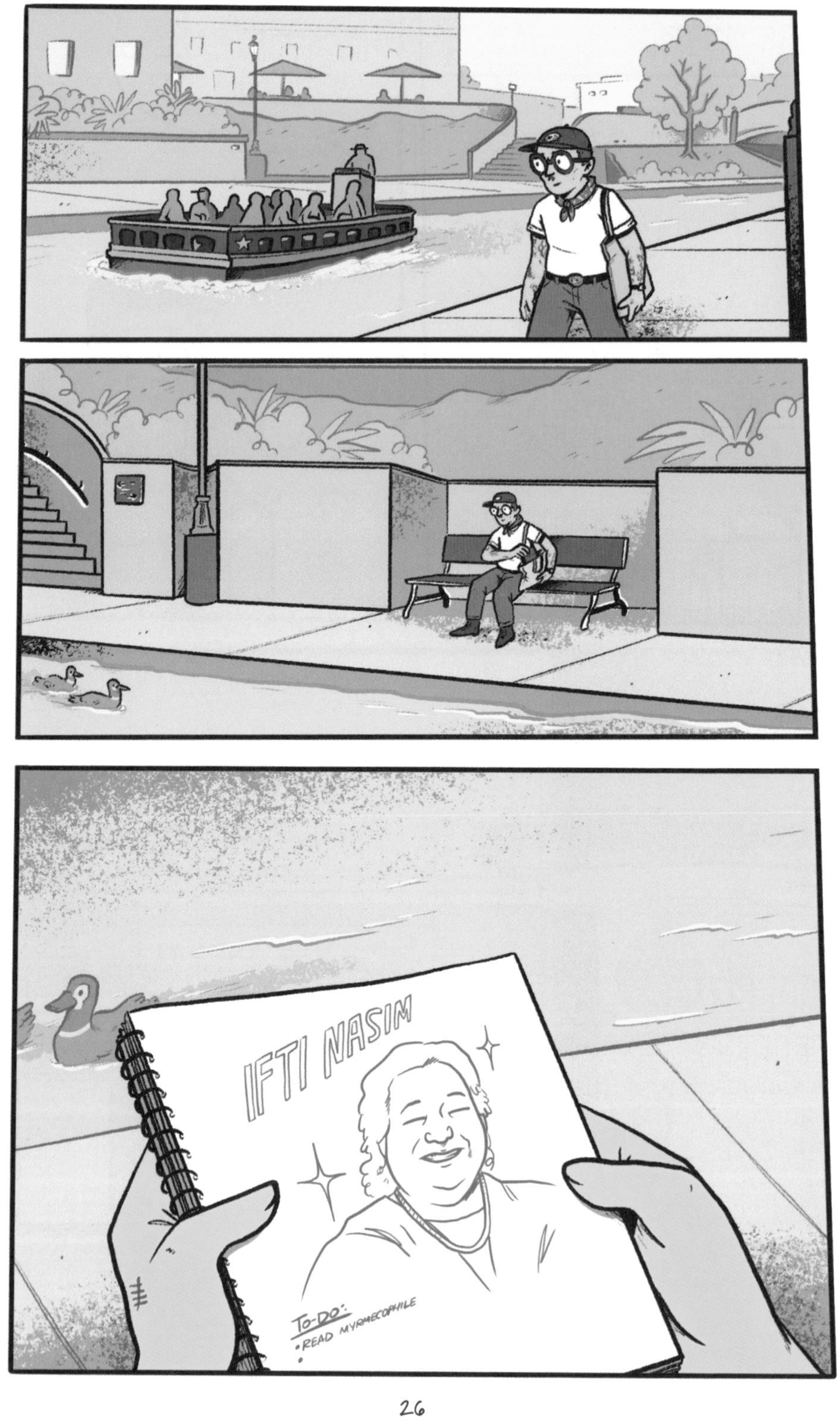
IFTI NASIM
TO-DO:
• READ MYRMECOPHILE
•

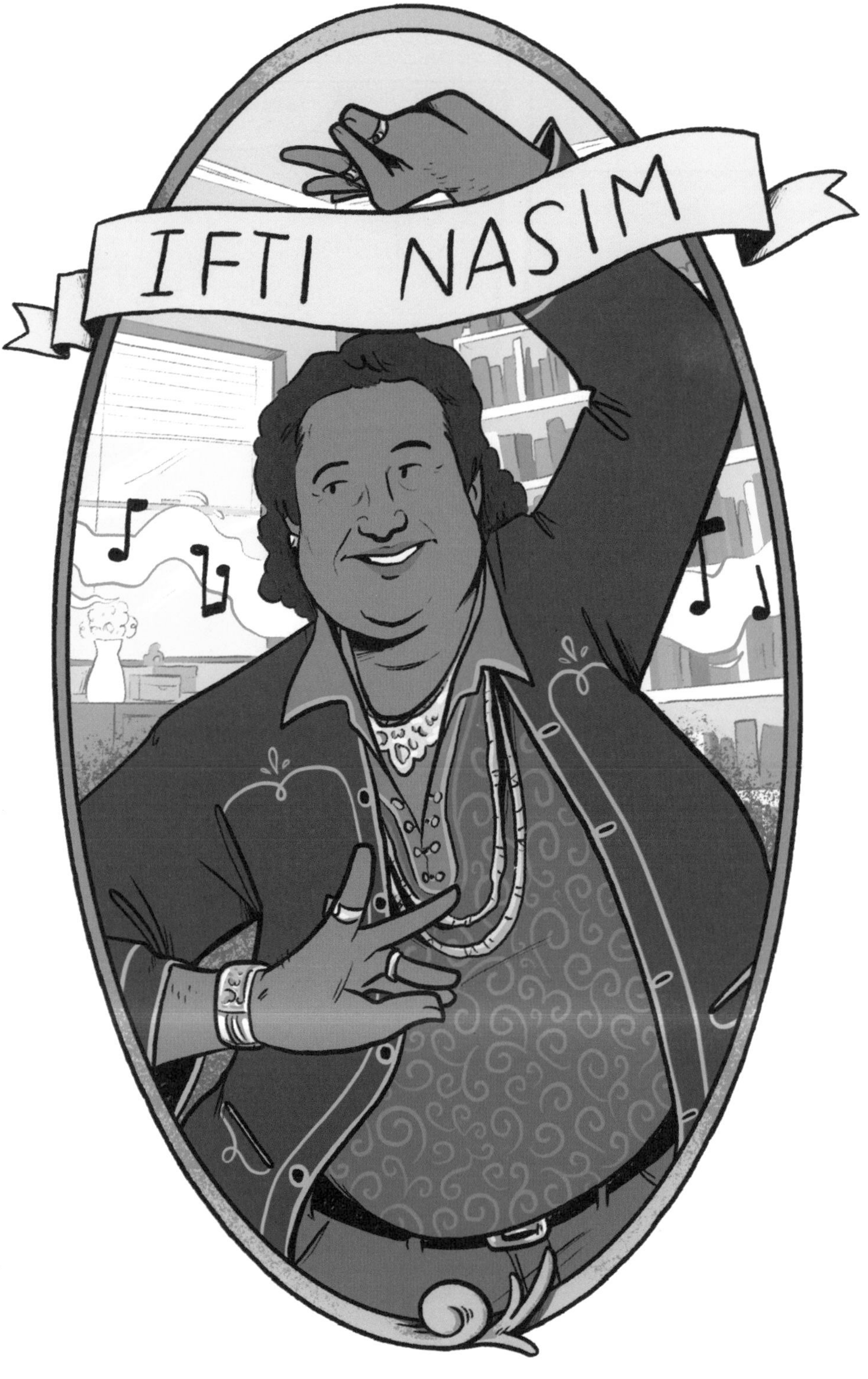
IFTI NASIM

IFTI NASIM WAS BORN IN 1946 IN FAISALABAD, PAKISTAN, TO A LARGE FAMILY OF SEVEN KIDS. HIS FATHER WAS A NEWSPAPER OWNER AND HIS MOTHER DIED WHEN HE WAS A CHILD.

AS A BOY, IFTI HAD DREAMS OF BECOMING A KATHAK DANCER AND LOVED THE ARTS, ESPECIALLY POETRY.

HIS COMMUNITY AND FAMILY DIDN'T BELIEVE "REAL MEN" BECAME DANCERS. NEVERTHELESS, HE DANCED IN PRIVATE WITH HIS FRIENDS AND CONTINUED TO WRITE POETRY.

MUCH LIKE NANCY CÁRDENAS, IFTI BECAME AN ACTIVIST AT AN EARLY AGE. AT SIXTEEN, HE ATTENDED A POLITICALLY CHARGED PROTEST AGAINST THE PAKISTANI GOVERNMENT'S USE OF MARTIAL LAW.

HE RECITED A POEM HE WROTE IN OBJECTION TO THE GOVERNMENT'S MILITARY CONTROL AGAINST ITS CITIZENS. BUT OPPOSITION TO LAW AND RELIGION IN THE AREA CAME AT QUITE A HEFTY PRICE.

AND IFTI PAID FOR BEING AN OUTLAW.

BANG!

DURING HIS READING, A SOLDIER SHOT IFTI IN THE LEG, CAUSING PERMANENT DAMAGE. LUCKILY, SOMEONE PULLED HIM OUT OF THE SPRAY OF BULLETS BEFORE ANOTHER GOT HIM.

GAAAHHH!

HE UNSUCCESSFULLY ATTEMPTED TO HIDE HIS WOUNDS FROM HIS FATHER AND WAS BEDRIDDEN FOR SIX WHOLE MONTHS!

IF THIS TRAGEDY WASN'T ENOUGH, IFTI STRUGGLED WITH BEING GAY. HIS LOCAL MUSLIM COMMUNITY AND HIS FATHER SAW HOMOSEXUALITY AS SINFUL AND IMMORAL.

IFTI DIDN'T THINK HE'D SURVIVE PAST THE AGE OF 40; HE THOUGHT HE MAY KILL HIMSELF BEFORE THEN.

ONE DAY WHILE OUT RUNNING ERRANDS, IFTI BUMPED INTO A PSYCHIATRIST THAT HELPED HIM DEAL WITH HIS SUICIDAL THOUGHTS. IFTI CLAIMS THAT THE DOCTOR'S HELP, ALONGSIDE HIS POETRY WRITING, WAS A "COMPLETE CATHARSIS FOR MY SOUL."

IFTI'S FATHER ARRANGED FOR HIM TO MARRY AT AGE 21.

Welcome home, son, I want to introduce you to your new wife.

I cannot marry a woman, that's not true to who I am. I'd be living a double life! How do I get out of an arranged marriage?

A *LIFE* MAGAZINE ARTICLE ABOUT GAY PEOPLE LIVING HAPPILY IN THE U.S.A. PLAYED IN THE BACK OF IFTI'S MIND.

Father, I was thinking and I have a great idea if you'll support it financially.

How about I go to America for the best schooling there is, come back, and get a good-paying job to support my new family?

IFTI'S FATHER AGREED.

BUT A FEW MONTHS IN AMERICA TURNED INTO A YEAR, WHICH TURNED INTO DECADES, AND EVENTUALLY THE REST OF HIS LIFE.

IFTI WAS MOSTLY WITHOUT HIS FAMILY IN AMERICA.

BY 1974, HE WAS LIVING IN THE THICK OF CHICAGO'S GAY SCENE.

IFTI WAS INTIMIDATED TO GO INTO GAY BARS AT FIRST; HE WASN'T SURE HOW HE'D FIT IN AS A YOUNG, QUEER PAKISTANI IMMIGRANT.

THERE WEREN'T MANY OTHER SOUTH ASIAN MEN IN THE GAY SCENE, BUT IFTI WAS ABLE TO TAKE UP SPACE AND FINALLY FIND HIS FUTURE LIFE PARTNER, PREM.

Martini, please!

IFTI DRESSED IN FLAMBOYANT AND COLORFUL CLOTHING, FUR COATS, AND WORE TONS OF GOLD JEWELRY.

TO FUND HIS POETRY CAREER, HE SOLD CARS. HE WAS THE TOP ROLLS-ROYCE AND MERCEDES BENZ SALESMAN AT THE DEALERSHIP.

Well, Mary, if you're looking for storage, the 450SL is the way to go.

Would you pop the trunk so I can check it out?

Oh, honey, do it yourself. I just got my nails done.

LEGEND HAS IT THAT HE DROVE A GOLD CAR AND ONCE SOLD A VEHICLE TO OPRAH WINFREY.

HE MIGHT HAVE BEEN OVER THE TOP IN LOOKS AND VIBRANT IN SPEECH, BUT IFTI WAS A FAIRLY PRIVATE PERSON.

IFTI WROTE POETRY IN THE URDU, PUNJABI, AND ENGLISH LANGUAGES.

HIS MOST FAMOUS WORK IS A BOOK OF POETRY TITLED **NARMAN**, WHICH IS BELIEVED TO BE THE FIRST PUBLICATION IN THE URDU LANGUAGE WITH DIRECT ALLUSIONS TO QUEER LONGING AND DESIRE.

IFTI HAD A CLOSE AND PERSONAL RELATIONSHIP TO HIS GOD AND FELT THE NEED TO JUSTIFY HIS SEXUALITY.

My father
If I am exactly like you then why my sexual preference is so much different from yours?

NARMAN WAS MET WITH FAIRLY MIXED REVIEWS. SOME SAW IT AS AN ABOMINATION TO GOD WHILE OTHERS LEARNED FROM IT THAT HOMOSEXUALITY IS NORMAL.

God wouldn't have created me if he didn't want me to lead a happy and fulfilled life.

God doesn't create trash.

IN 1983, IFTI CO-FOUNDED SANGAT CHICAGO, AN ORGANIZATION THAT SUPPORTED THE LOCAL SOUTH ASIAN QUEER COMMUNITY OF CHICAGO AND SURROUNDING AREAS.

THE NAME TAKES ITS MEANING FROM THE SANSKRIT WORD SANGAT, MEANING TOGETHERNESS OR COMMUNITY.

Ifti, it's always a good day when I get to see you!

ONE OF SANGAT CHICAGO'S MOST IMPORTANT ACTIONS INCLUDED HIRING IMMIGRATION LAWYERS TO FIGHT FOR ITS MEMBERS. EVERY ONE OF THEM SOUGHT ASYLUM IN AMERICA TO ESCAPE PERSECUTION FOR THEIR SEXUALITIES.

They're lost when they come here and find out they're homosexuals. They are a minority within a minority.

And that's the damn truth!

UNFORTUNATELY SANGAT NO LONGER EXISTS, BUT SOME OF ITS ROOTS ARE STILL PART OF THE CHICAGO QUEER COMMUNITY. A FEW OF THE GROUP MEMBERS THAT ARE STILL AROUND TODAY SPEAK FONDLY OF IFTI AND THE WORK THE ORGANIZATION DID.

IFTI WAS INDUCTED INTO THE CHICAGO GAY AND LESBIAN HALL OF FAME IN 1996 FOR HIS WORK ON SANGAT CHICAGO.

HE ALSO WROTE A WEEKLY COLUMN FOR A PAKISTANI-AMERICAN NEWSPAPER AND HOSTED A RADIO SHOW, BOTH OF WHICH HE USED TO SPEAK OUT AGAINST HARMFUL RELIGIOUS POLICIES TOWARD WOMEN AND QUEER PEOPLE.

IN 2003, IFTI SUFFERED A NEARLY FATAL HEART ATTACK.

HE DROVE HIMSELF TO THE HOSPITAL IN HIS GOLD CAR.

IT IS SAID THAT WHILE IN THE HOSPITAL FOR HIS HEART ATTACK, A MALE NURSE HIT ON HIM, TO WHICH HE RESPONDED...

Not now, please.

BY 2011, IFTI HAD PROVEN HIMSELF WRONG:

HE DIDN'T DIE BEFORE THE AGE OF 40 FROM SUICIDE.

HE LIVED TO THE AGE OF 64, WHEN HE DIED BY A SECOND HEART ATTACK, LEAVING BEHIND PREM, HIS PARTNER OF THREE DECADES, HIS FRIENDS, CHOSEN FAMILY, COMMUNITY, AND A MASSIVE AMOUNT OF WRITING.

IFTI ONCE SAID,

"NO ONE MADE ME GAY. I WAS BORN THIS WAY."

IFTI FOUND WAYS TO LIVE UNASHAMEDLY BY SEEKING REFUGE IN ART AND COMMUNITY.

I'VE LEARNED FROM IFTI THAT I CAN CHANGE WHATEVER MAKES IT HARD TO BE MYSELF, AND TO FIND COMMUNITIES OR CHOSEN FAMILY THAT WILL SUPPORT ME.

Oh, cool, it's only 11. I still have time to kill before meeting Max.

I HAVEN'T BEEN ON THIS PLANET FOR A LONG TIME, BUT I KNOW THAT IT CAN SUCK TO BE ALIVE SOMETIMES.

I, LIKE IFTI AND SO MANY QUEER AND TRANSGENDER PEOPLE, HAVE DEALT WITH SUICIDAL THOUGHTS AND ATTEMPTS.

EVEN WHEN LIFE FEELS HOPELESS, THERE IS ALWAYS HELP.

PLEASE REFER TO THE HELP AND RESOURCES SECTION IN THE BACK OF THE BOOK IF YOU'RE STRUGGLING WITH SUICIDAL THOUGHTS.

I HAVE BEEN ABLE TO GET HELP AND AM THANKFUL. LIKE IFTI, I WANT TO STICK AROUND FOR EXTRA MOMENTS OF JOY. IF I HAD DIED YOUNG, I WOULD NOT HAVE BEEN ABLE TO CONTINUE CREATING MY ART.

IFTI REMINDS ME THAT MY PASSIONS CAN HELP KEEP ME AND OTHERS ALIVE, AND THAT I CAN DO INCREDIBLE THINGS.

HOPEFULLY HIS LIFE STORY DOES THE SAME FOR YOU.

THE ARTS HAVE TRULY SAVED ME. I HONESTLY DON'T KNOW WHAT I WOULD'VE DONE WITHOUT SOME OF THE BANDS THAT I LOVE.

I LISTENED TO MY CHEMICAL ROMANCE AS A MIDDLE SCHOOLER AND REMEMBER FEELING LESS LONELY AS I GRAPPLED WITH MY SEXUALITY, RELIGION, AND FAMILY LIFE. THAT BAND TAUGHT ME THAT I WAS NOT THE ONLY PERSON THAT FELT DEPRESSED AND ANGRY.

I FOUND PEOPLE ONLINE WHO LIKED THIS BAND AS MUCH AS I DO, AND MANY OF THEM WERE ALSO QUEER. SOME OF THESE PEOPLE I STILL TALK TO TODAY, YEARS LATER.

THAT WAS MY FIRST CHOSEN FAMILY.

41

AT THE TIME, MANY OF MY INTERNET FRIENDS AND I WERE STUCK IN THE CLOSET.

LIVING IN THE SHADOWS SEEMS TO BE A SHARED QUEER EXPERIENCE.

SOME OF US HIDE ONLINE IN FORUMS AND GROUP CHATS, OR MEET BEHIND CLOSED DOORS, MASKING OUR LOVE IN PUBLIC TO MAINTAIN OUR SAFETY.

OBVIOUSLY THERE ARE SOME PEOPLE THAT HAVE NEVER FELT THE NEED TO HIDE, BUT FOR MANY OF US IT'S A STRUGGLE.

IT'S STILL RARE THAT I HEAR QUEER PEOPLE DISCUSSING THEIR ISSUES, FEARS, RELATIONSHIPS, AND STRUGGLES WITH IDENTITY IN PUBLIC.

BUT THAT COULD BE BECAUSE OF WHERE I LIVE. THE FEAR OF BEING EXPOSED TO A VIOLENT BIGOT LOOMS LARGE.

MANY PEOPLE DON'T KNOW THAT ONE OF THE ORIGINAL INNOVATORS OF ROCK 'N' ROLL WAS A QUEER BLACK WOMAN,

A WOMAN WHO RETREATED BACK INTO THE CLOSET FROM TIME TO TIME AND MET WITH LOVERS BEHIND CLOSED DOORS. SHE WAS NEVER FULLY OUT.

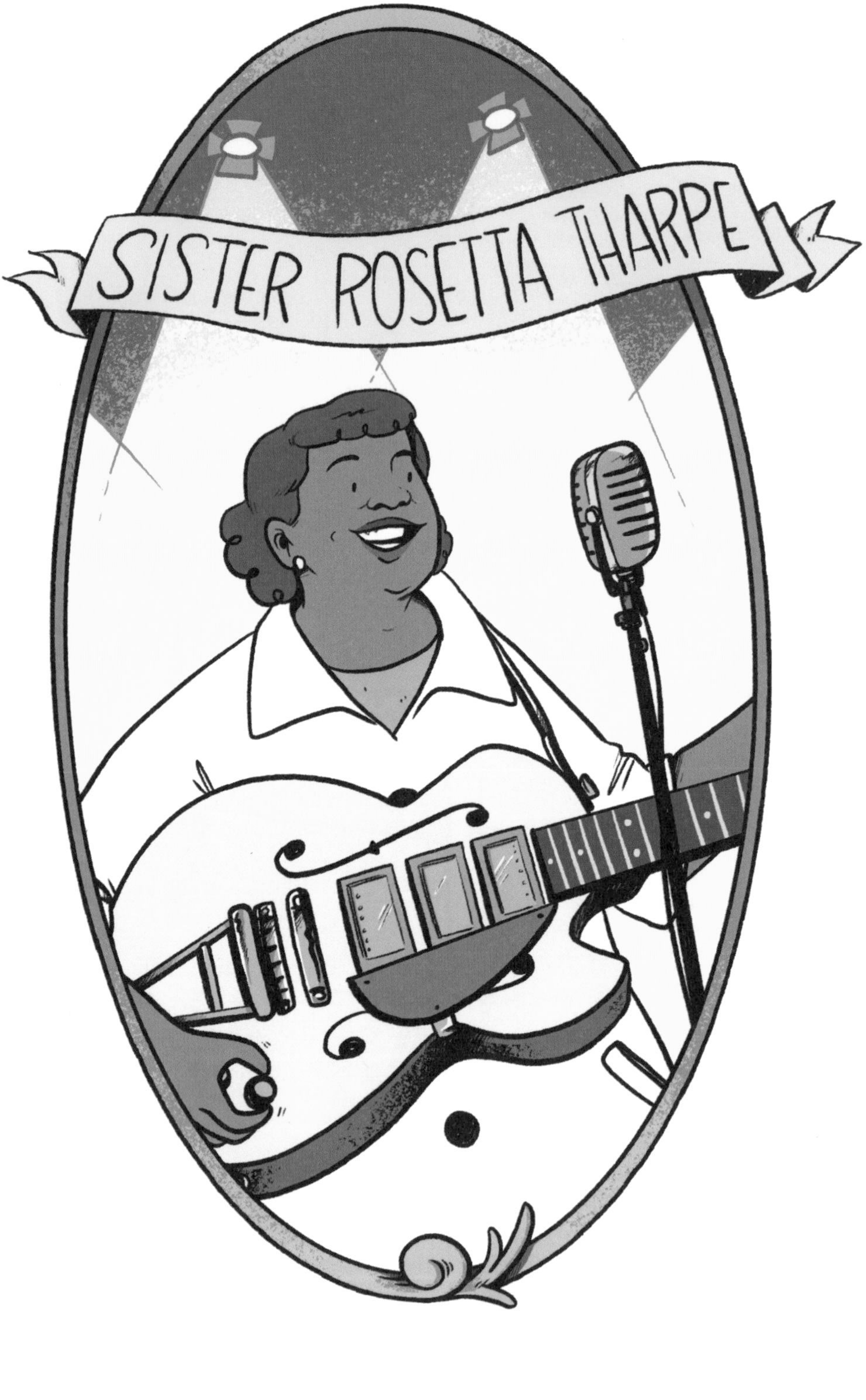
SISTER ROSETTA THARPE

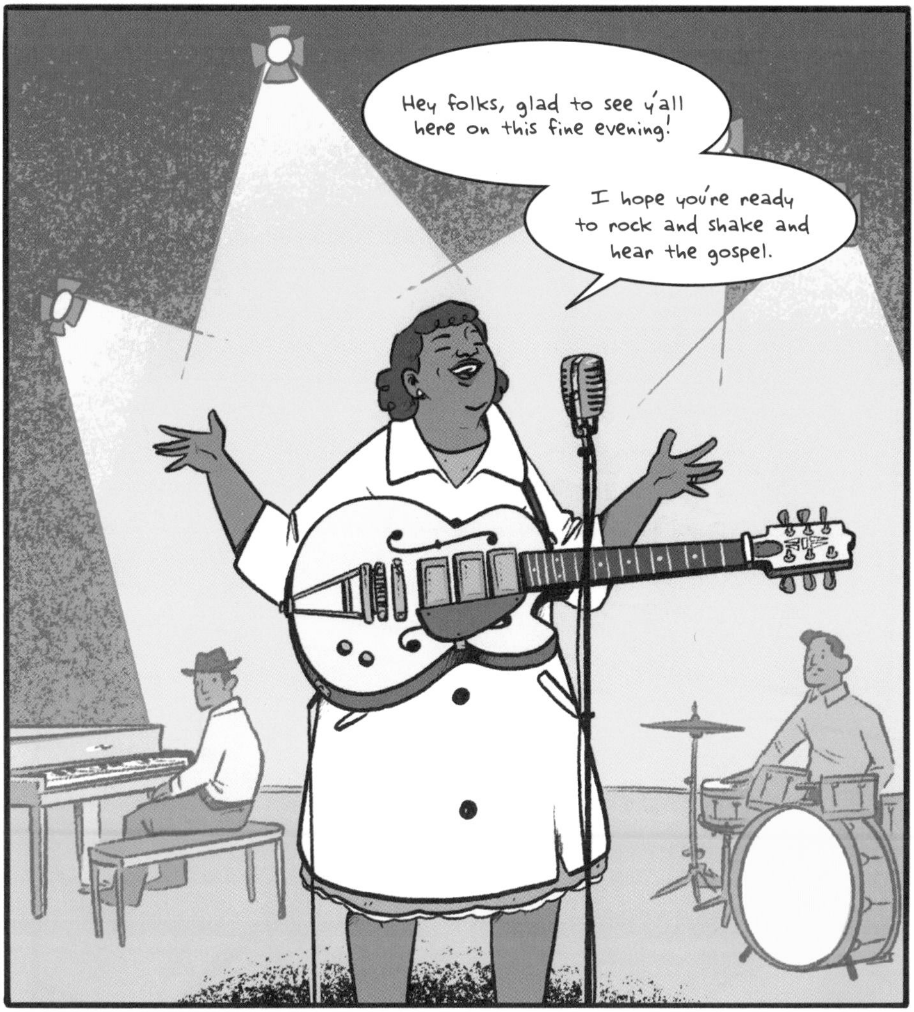
Hey folks, glad to see y'all here on this fine evening!
I hope you're ready to rock and shake and hear the gospel.

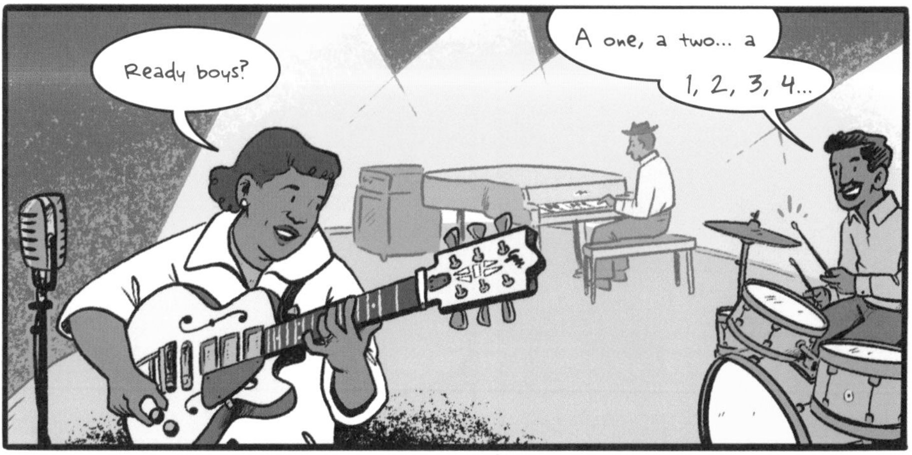
Ready boys?
A one, a two... a
1, 2, 3, 4...

SISTER ROSETTA THARPE WAS AN ICONIC GOSPEL-SINGING POWERHOUSE AND QUEER BLACK WOMAN.

SHE WAS BORN ROSETTA NUBIN ON MARCH 20, 1915, IN COTTON PLANT, ARKANSAS.

HER MOTHER, KATIE BELL NUBIN, WAS A GOSPEL MUSICIAN AND EVANGELIST PREACHER FOR THE CHURCH OF GOD IN CHRIST.

Why don't you rock my soul?

WOMEN SERVED IN THE CHURCH AS SUNDAY SCHOOL INSTRUCTORS, EVANGELISTS, AND MUSIC TEACHERS.

In the bosom of Abraham!

AS PART OF AN EVANGELICAL CONCERT TOUR, ROSETTA BEGAN SINGING GOSPEL AND PLAYING GUITAR WITH HER MOTHER FOR LARGE CROWDS ACROSS THE AMERICAN SOUTH.

EVEN AT SIX YEARS OLD, ROSETTA WAS THE STAR OF THE TROUPE. SHE WAS CALLED A "SINGING AND GUITAR PLAYING MIRACLE."

TONIGHT! 6PM

THE SINGING & GUITAR PLAYING MIRACLE

IN PERSON!

Momma, how many people do you think will show up tonight?

Hard to tell, Rosetta, but it sure is gonna be a crowd.

BY THE MID-1920S, ROSETTA AND HER MOTHER SETTLED IN CHICAGO WHERE THEY CONTINUED TO PERFORM AT VARIOUS CHURCHES AND CONVENTIONS.

ROSETTA BEGAN TO FUSE DELTA BLUES, NEW ORLEANS JAZZ, AND GOSPEL MUSIC, CRAFTING HER UNIQUE GUITAR STYLE.

ROSETTA MARRIED A CHURCH OF GOD IN CHRIST PREACHER, THOMAS J. THORPE, WHEN SHE WAS 19 YEARS OLD.

THEIR MARRIAGE WAS SHORT-LIVED. AFTER THEY SPLIT, ROSETTA ALTERED HER MARRIED NAME, "THORPE" TO "THARPE" INSTEAD OF RETURNING TO HER MAIDEN NAME.

DURING HER TIME IN CHICAGO, SHE GAINED QUITE A REPUTATION AS A MUSICAL PRODIGY. AT THE TIME, BLACK FEMALE GUITARISTS WHO RECEIVED RECOGNITION WERE FEW AND FAR IN BETWEEN.

IN 1938, SHE AND HER MOTHER PACKED UP THEIR BELONGINGS AND HEADED TO NEW YORK CITY, READY TO MAKE IT **BIG!**

ROSETTA SIGNED WITH DECCA RECORDS AND CUT FOUR SONGS WITH THEM, WHICH INSTANTLY BECAME HITS!

Now won't you hear me singing. Hear the words that I'm saying.

IN THE SAME YEAR, SHE PERFORMED AT CARNEGIE HALL IN JOHN HAMMOND'S "SPIRITUALS TO SWING" CONCERT, A GOSPEL SET.

Who woulda' thought a small town Arkansas girl like me could play in such a beautiful place as Carnegie Hall? Wow!

AT THE TIME, IT WAS UNUSUAL TO PLAY GOSPEL FOR NONRELIGIOUS CROWDS, ESPECIALLY ALONGSIDE THE JAZZ AND BLUES MUSICIANS ON THE BILL.

THROUGHOUT THE 1940s, ROSETTA KEPT A DEMANDING TOUR SCHEDULE, PLAYING IN CHURCHES AS WELL AS SECULAR NIGHT CLUBS TO RACIALLY MIXED CROWDS.

AND IN THAT SAME DECADE, SHE MET MARIE KNIGHT.

Oh, my stars...

Who is this angel playing on stage?

THE PAIR ENTERED INTO A CLANDESTINE ROMANTIC RELATIONSHIP ON TOUR TOGETHER.

53

PEOPLE WHO KNEW ROSETTA REVEALED THAT SHE WAS QUEER WHEN A BIOGRAPHY ABOUT HER CAME OUT IN 2007.

THEY ALSO SUSPECT ROSETTA MIGHT'VE MARRIED NUMEROUS MEN TO COVER UP THIS FACT.

ONE SUCH MARRIAGE IN 1951 TO HER MANAGER, RUSSELL MORRISON, WAS HELD AT:

GRIFFITH STADIUM, WASHINGTON, D.C.

THE WEDDING-TURNED-CONCERT WAS GRANDIOSE, WITNESSED BY A CROWD OF OVER 20,000 PEOPLE, AND WAS LATER PRESSED INTO VINYL.

PERHAPS THE LARGE-SCALE CEREMONY WAS AIMED AT CONCEALING ROSETTA'S SEXUAL IDENTITY.

IT'S STILL UNKNOWN WHETHER THE WEDDING WAS FOR PUBLICITY ALONE.

ROSETTA CONTINUED TO TOUR AMERICA AND EVENTUALLY EUROPE. SHE PLAYED ALONGSIDE MANY INCREDIBLE MUSICIANS.

SHE WAS EVEN ABLE TO BUY HER OWN HOME.

ROSETTA WAS LEGENDARY FOR OUTPLAYING MANY MEN ON GUITAR, MAKING HER THE GODMOTHER OF ROCK 'N' ROLL.

SHE CONTINUED TO WORK FOR THREE MORE YEARS UNTIL SHE DIED OF A STROKE IN 1973 THE NIGHT BEFORE A RECORDING SESSION.

WHEN IT CAME TO HER CRAFT ROSETTA WAS WITHOUT BOUNDARIES.

Why don't you rock my soul, in the bosom of Abraham.

HER UNIQUE STYLE INSPIRED EARLY PIONEERS OF ROCK 'N' ROLL AND COUNTLESS OTHERS.

ELVIS PRESLEY

LITTLE RICHARD

ROSETTA WAS INDUCTED INTO THE ROCK 'N' ROLL HALL OF FAME IN CLEVELAND ON MAY 5, 2018. MANY, MANY YEARS AFTER ELVIS PRESLEY AND LITTLE RICHARD.

Rosetta Tharpe

Oh, these kids and rock 'n' roll— this is just sped up rhythm and blues.

I've been doing that forever.

I FIRST HEARD ABOUT ROSETTA ON **NPR** AND IMMEDIATELY FELL IN LOVE WITH HER MUSIC.

WHEN I LEARNED SHE WAS QUEER, I WENT DOWN A RABBIT HOLE OF RESEARCH, FINDING OUT ABOUT OTHER QUEER PEOPLE I HAD NEVER HEARD OF.

IN MY RESEARCH, I HAVE LEARNED THAT THE GENDER SPECTRUM IS NOT A NEW CONCEPT. MANY PEOPLE AT CHURCH OR IN MY FAMILY HAVE TRIED TO CONVINCE ME THAT GENDER IS BINARY, AND ALL TALK OTHERWISE IS JUST A PASSING FAD. SOME INDIGENOUS CULTURES ON THE NORTH AMERICAN CONTINENT, LIKE THE ZUNI, LAKOTA, NAVAJO, OJIBWE, BLACKFOOT, AND CREE, HAVE ACKNOWLEDGED THE AMBIGUITIES OF GENDER FOR CENTURIES.

A FEW OF THESE TRIBES HAVE ADOPTED THE MODERN TERM "TWO-SPIRIT" FOR THOSE THAT FALL OUTSIDE OF A TWO-GENDER BINARY.

IT SEEMS TO ME THAT A LOT OF WESTERN CULTURES VIEW LIFE WITH LITTLE WIGGLE ROOM: RIGHT AND WRONG, BLACK AND WHITE, MALE AND FEMALE, GOOD AND EVIL.

SOME OF THE IGNORANCE I'VE EXPERIENCED SURROUNDING GENDER ALSO STEMS FROM THE FACT THAT MY SCHOOL TEXTBOOKS LEFT OUT COMPLEX NOTIONS OF GENDER.

WE'RE ESPECIALLY BAD ABOUT LEAVING IMPORTANT HISTORY OUT OF THE CORE CURRICULUM HERE IN THE AMERICAN SOUTH.

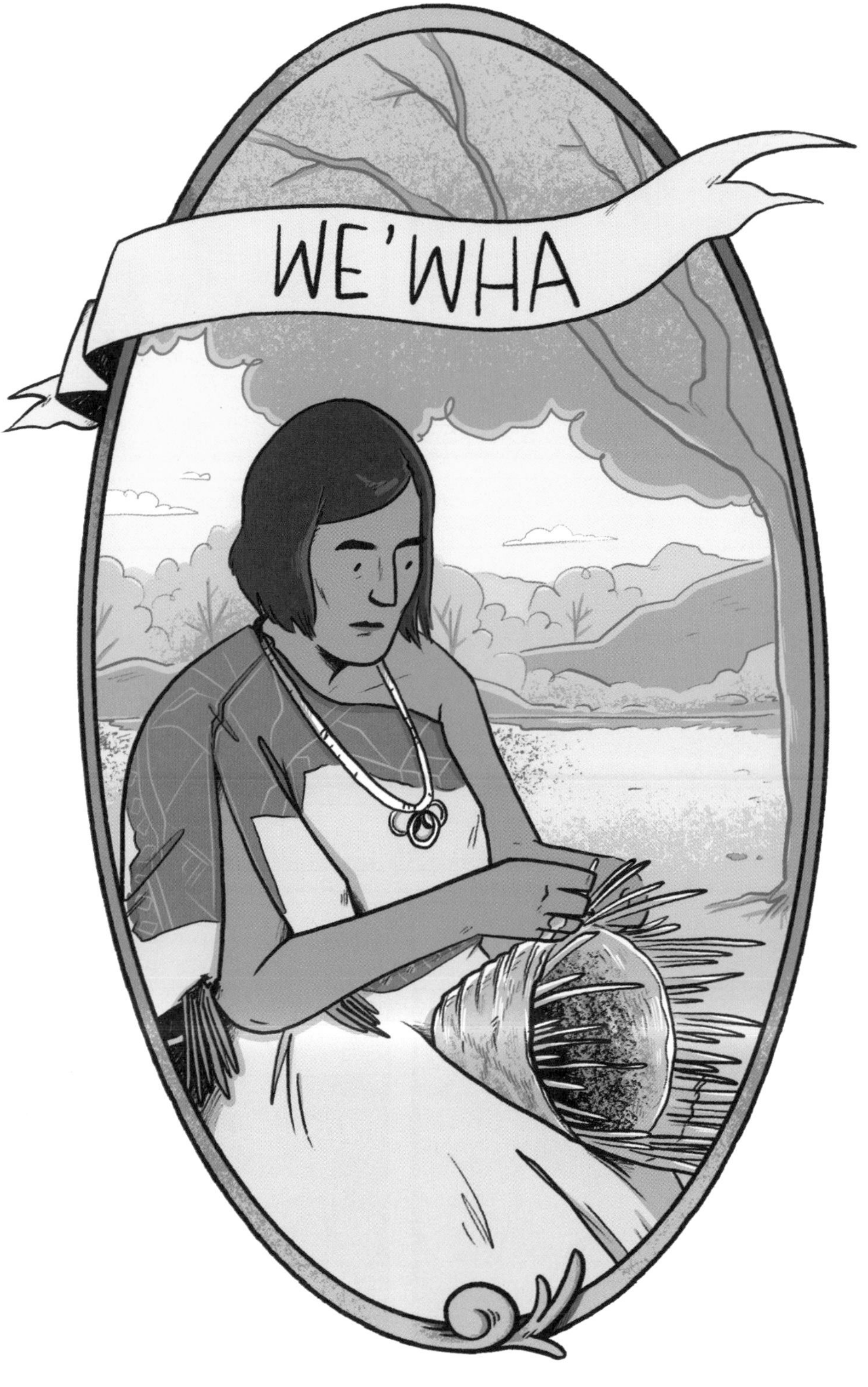
WE'WHA

WE'WHA WAS BORN IN 1849 TO THE ZUNI TRIBE,

IN ONE OF THE OLDEST CONTINUALLY INHABITED VILLAGES OF PRESENT-DAY NEW MEXICO.

IN 1853, AFTER A PARTY OF AMERICAN SETTLERS PASSED THROUGH, AN OUTBREAK OF SMALLPOX DEVASTATED THE VILLAGE.

WHEN BOTH OF WE'WHA'S PARENTS DIED OF THIS NEW DISEASE, WE'WHA'S AUNT TOOK OVER AS CARETAKER.

You and I will stay strong, dear We'Wha.

THE ZUNI PEOPLE ARE MATRILINEAL. THEY BELONG TO EXTENDED FAMILIES, CALLED CLANS, AND TRACE THEIR DESCENT THROUGH THEIR MOTHERS. HOUSES ARE OWNED BY THE ELDEST WOMAN IN THE FAMILY AND MEN LIVE IN THEIR OWN HOMES.

ASSIGNED MALE AT BIRTH, WE'WHA TOOK PART IN ZUNI CEREMONIES FOR BOYS AT AGE TWELVE.

AT SOME POINT, TRIBAL ELDERS RECOGNIZED LHAMANA* TRAITS IN WE'WHA, SO THEY CONTINUED RELIGIOUS TRAINING WITH FEMALE RELATIVES.

*Two-Spirit in traditional Zuni culture

IN THE ZUNI TRADITION, KACHINAS, OR KOKKO, ARE MASKED DEITIES REPRESENTING TRIBAL ANCESTORS.

ZUNI STORIES TELL OF A KACHINA NAMED KO'LHAMANA, WHO WAS CAPTIVE IN A WAR BETWEEN THE ZUNI'S ANCESTORS, WHO WERE FARMERS, AND AN ENEMY PEOPLE WHO WERE HUNTERS.

THE KO'LHAMANA KACHINA REPRESENTS A THIRD GENDER ROLE ABLE TO BRIDGE OPPOSITIONS LIKE HUNTING AND FARMING, AND MEN AND WOMEN.

TWO-SPIRIT PEOPLE CHOOSE THE PRONOUNS THEY PREFER,

AND THE ZUNI LANGUAGE DOESN'T INCLUDE THIRD-PERSON PRONOUNS EQUIVALENT TO THE WORDS "SHE," "HE," AND "THEY" IN ENGLISH.

I'VE USED WE-WHA'S NAME IN PLACE OF PRONOUNS SO FAR, AND "THEY" ONLY WHEN AN ALTERNATIVE DOESN'T IMMEDIATELY PRESENT ITSELF.

THE U.S. GOVERNMENT SENT WHITE MINISTERS TO "CONVERT" THE TRIBE TO CHRISTIANITY. BY 1888, THEY LEFT THE PUEBLO WITHOUT MAKING MUCH IMPACT ON ZUNI BELIEFS.

THE U.S. GOVERNMENT ALSO SENT SMITHSONIAN ETHNOLOGIST MATILDA COXE STEVENSON TO DOCUMENT AND STUDY THE TRIBE.

MATILDA INTRODUCED COMMERCIAL LAUNDRY SOAP TO THE TRIBE, AND WE'WHA STARTED WASHING LARGE QUANTITIES OF SOLDIERS' CLOTHES AT FORT WINGATE NEAR GALLUP, NEW MEXICO, FOR MONEY.

WE'WHA SOON EXPANDED THE ENDEAVOR TO WASH FOR WHITE SETTLERS, TOO.

WE'WHA WAS ONE OF THE BEST ZUNI POTTERS, AND MATILDA PAID THEM TO MAKE POTS THAT ARE NOW IN THE COLLECTION OF THE NATIONAL MUSEUM OF NATURAL HISTORY IN WASHINGTON, D.C.

Someone catalogued these pieces individually instead of altogether. Could you tell me if all of these items make up a loom?

WE'WHA SPENT SIX MONTHS WORKING IN WASHINGTON, D.C., ON LOOMS, ALWAYS FOLLOWING STRICT RELIGIOUS PROTOCOLS OF THE ZUNI PEOPLE.

WHILE WE'WHA FELT THEIR WORK WAS IMPORTANT FOR THE PRESERVATION OF ZUNI CULTURE,

ZUNI POTT

IT MIGHT BE NOTED THAT THE U.S. GOVERNMENT DID NOT SEEM TOO CONCERNED WITH THE WELL-BEING OF INDIGENOUS PEOPLE THEMSELVES.

FOUR YEARS LATER, WE'WHA LAY DYING OF HEART DISEASE. THE BOW PRIEST WAS SUMMONED TO HELP HEAL WE'WHA OF THEIR AILMENTS.

UNFORTUNATELY, HE WAS UNABLE TO STOP THE SPREAD OF THE DISEASE.

WE'WHA MOVED BETWEEN OPPOSING WORLDS IN THEIR LIFETIME, EVEN AT ONE POINT MEETING WITH THE PRESIDENT OF THE UNITED STATES GROVER CLEVELAND.

BUT IN THE END, WE'WHA DIED AT THE AGE OF 49 DUE TO HEART FAILURE.

AND WE'WHA'S LAST WORDS WERE TO SAY GOODBYE TO ALL OF THEIR FRIENDS IN WASHINGTON, D.C.

I NEVER LEARNED ABOUT TWO-SPIRIT PEOPLE IN SCHOOL, WHICH IS NO SURPRISE.

THE LONG AND VIOLENT ERASURE OF INDIGENOUS CULTURES FROM AMERICAN HISTORY CONTINUES TODAY.

WELL BEFORE THE MODERN-DAY TERM "TRANSGENDER" EXISTED, THE ZUNI'S LHAMANA PEOPLE SERVED A VITAL ROLE IN THE COMMUNITY.

PEOPLE EXISTED BEYOND THE GENDER BINARY IN MESOPOTAMIA, ANCIENT EGYPT, THE HIJRA PEOPLE OF SOUTH ASIA, SCYTHIAN PEOPLE, THE MAHU OF HAWAII AND TAHITI, INDONESIA'S BUGIS PEOPLE, AND EVEN IN JUDAISM.

END WHITE SUPREMACY

NO MONUMENT TO MURDER

CLUNK!

CHRISTOPHER COLUMBUS

TODAY, ACTIVISTS CONTINUE TO DISMANTLE MONUMENTS OF WHITE COLONISTS THAT HURT INDIGENOUS COMMUNITIES IN THE U.S.

The statue is finally gone!

Sorry I missed ya, let's do coffee soon.

Celebration barbacoa and Big Red at my house, let's go y'all!

Last one to the car does the dishes! We'll give you a head start, Ma.

I'VE ALWAYS BEEN A CURIOUS PERSON, AND I TEND TO DIVE INTO SUBJECTS THAT INTEREST ME WITH HYPER-FOCUS.

ON MANY OCCASIONS, FERVENT RESEARCH HAS HELPED QUELL MY ANXIETY.

RESEARCH IS MY SAVING GRACE, AND IT LED ME TO EVERY PERSON WHO INSPIRES ME IN THIS BOOK.

library entrance

Oh, hey, Shelby! The book that you requested just came in this morning.

Well then, it is the perfect day to come to the library!

Thank you.

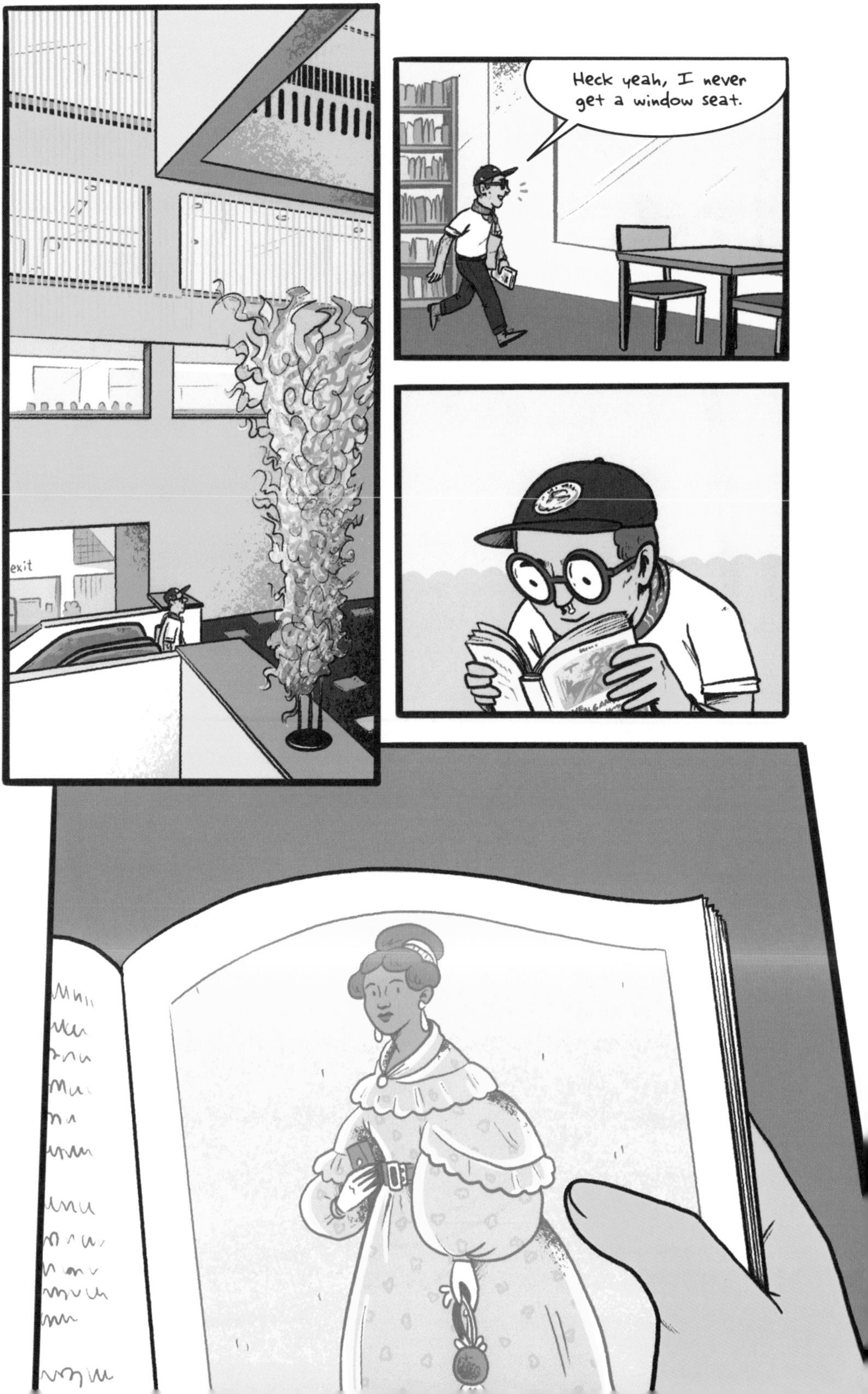
exit
Heck yeah, I never get a window seat.

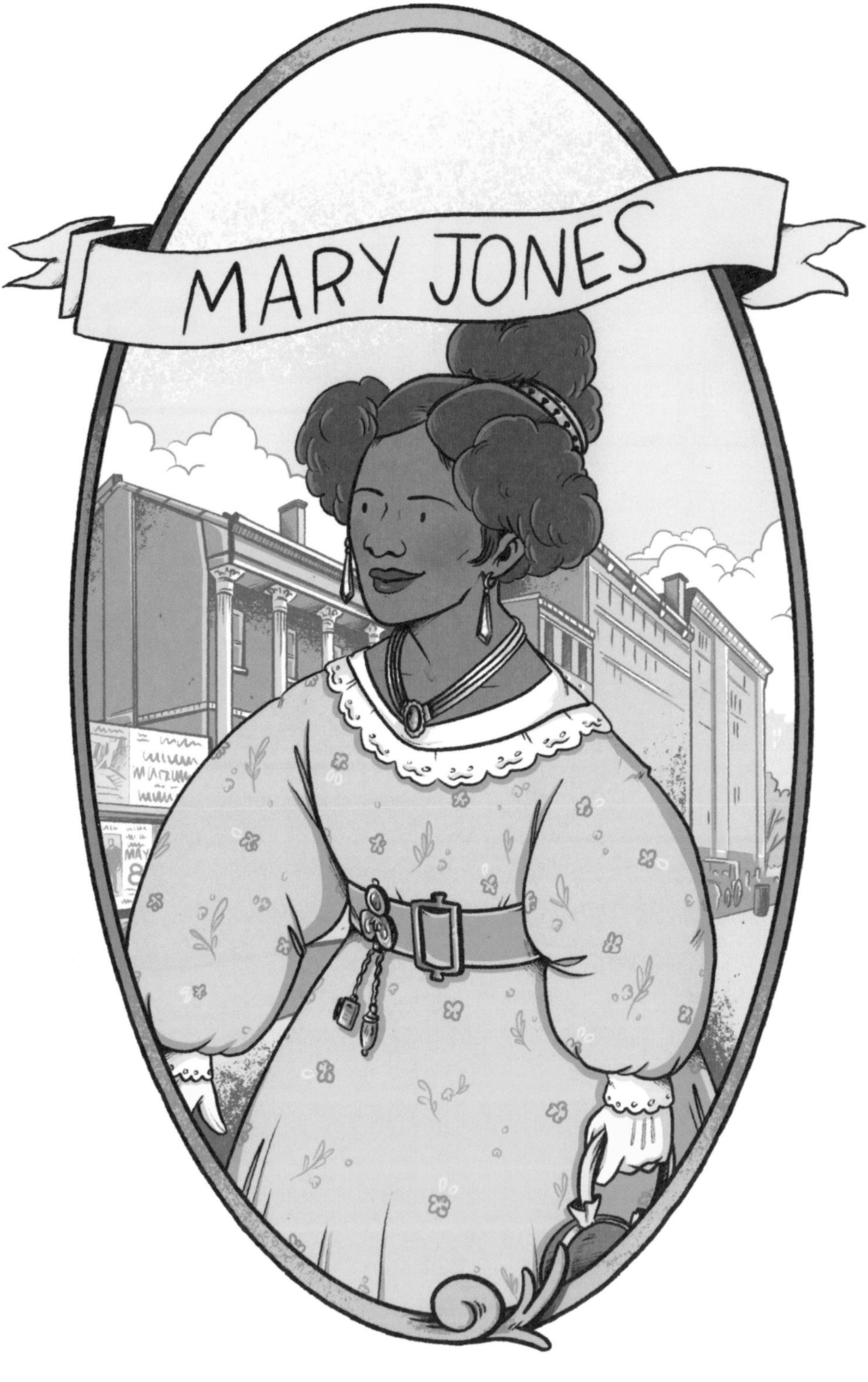
MARY JONES

MOST OF THE DETAILS OF MARY JONES'S LIFE ARE LOST

THIS IS COMMON AMONG BLACK AMERICANS WHOSE ANCESTORS WERE ENSLAVED. THE U.S. CENSUS DIDN'T BEGIN RECORDING ITS AFRICAN POPULATION UNTIL 1870.

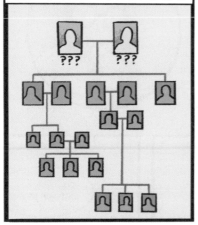

THIS INEXCUSABLE HOLE IN AMERICAN HISTORY IS KNOWN BY GENEALOGISTS AS "THE BRICK WALL."

BY 1780, MORE THAN 10,000 FORMERLY ENSLAVED BLACK PEOPLE LIVED IN NEW YORK CITY. MARY JONES WAS BORN AROUND 1803 TO FORMERLY ENSLAVED PARENTS. ASSIGNED MALE AT BIRTH UNDER A DIFFERENT NAME, MARY PREFERRED TO GO BY ANOTHER MONIKER WHEN SHE BECAME AN ADULT.

Today, referring to the birth name of someone who has since chosen another is called "dead naming." It is disrespectful to refer to a person's dead name, and we aren't about to do that here!

GENERAL STORE

If that's all for ya, it will be 20 cents, ma'am.

set...

Well, thank you, Mary.

Oh, you can call me Mary.

FROM THE FEW RECORDS THAT EXIST ABOUT MARY, LIKE NEWSPAPER ACCOUNTS AND COURT AFFIDAVITS, I BELIEVE THAT SHE WAS IN THE MILITARY AND SPENT SOME TIME IN NEW ORLEANS.

THERE, AND IN NEW YORK, MARY FOUND WORK AS A MAID AND CHEF, OFTEN IN BROTHELS WHERE SHE TOOK CARE OF THE SEX WORKERS WHO LIVED THERE.

SHE WORKED THE BROTHEL DOOR, GREETED PATRONS AND COLLECTED PAYMENTS, AND SOMETIMES DID SEX WORK HERSELF.

SHE WOULD OCCASIONALLY STEAL WALLETS FROM MEN WHO CAME TO SEE HER.

IF NOT FOR HER PICKPOCKETING AND SUBSEQUENT ARRESTS, WE MAY NOT HAVE ANY RECORDS OF MARY'S EXISTENCE AT ALL.

WHILE WORKING IN BROTHELS, MARY'S FRIENDS AND COWORKERS ENCOURAGED HER TO EXPRESS HER GENDER BY WEARING CLOTHING TRADITIONALLY MADE FOR WOMEN. SOON, SHE STARTED WEARING WOMEN'S CLOTHING IN PUBLIC, TOO.

That is such a gorgeous gown, Mary.

CONSIDERED A SECOND-CLASS CITIZEN FOR BEING BLACK, MARY ALSO EXPERIENCED SEXISM AS A WOMAN IN VICTORIAN SOCIETY.

STILL, SHE STARTED PASSING IN PUBLIC.

ON THE NIGHT OF JUNE 11, 1836 WHEN MARY WAS WALKING DOWN BLEECKER STREET, A MAN NAMED ROBERT HASLEM APPROACHED HER TO SOLICIT SEX.

THE TWO OF THEM SLIPPED INTO A SECLUDED ALLEYWAY.

LATER, ROBERT WAS WALKING HOME AND REALIZED HIS WALLET, IN WHICH HE HAD $99, HAD BEEN REPLACED IN HIS POCKET WITH ANOTHER MAN'S WALLET.

Huh?

ROBERT FOUND THE OTHER WALLET'S OWNER, WHO AT FIRST DENIED IT WAS HIS BEFORE ADMITTING THAT HE TOO ENGAGED WITH MARY ON THE SAME NIGHT.

We've been swindled!

HE DIDN'T REPORT HIS MISSING WALLET TO THE AUTHORITIES FOR FEAR OF BEING ARRESTED FOR SOLICITING SEX.

THOUGH HE RISKED EXPOSING HIMSELF TO THE POLICE FOR THE SAME THING, ROBERT INSISTED ON REPORTING THE INCIDENT.

UNDERCOVER POLICE PATROLLED THE STREETS LOOKING FOR MARY, AND EVENTUALLY CAUGHT UP WITH HER ON THE BOWERY.

Where are you going at this time of night?

I am going home. Will you go too?

MARY TREATED THE MOMENT LIKE SHE WOULD WITH ANY CLIENT: SHE FOUND AN ALLEYWAY TO TAKE HIM TO.

WHEN MARY QUICKLY REALIZED SHE WAS WITH A COP, SHE TRIED TO DUMP THE STASH OF STOLEN WALLETS SHE HAD HIDDEN IN HER BRA.

AFTER HER ARREST, POLICE SEARCHED HER APARTMENT AND FOUND A NUMBER OF WALLETS AND TRINKETS BELONGING TO PROMINENT MEN IN THE CITY.

MARY WAS TRIED FOR GRAND LARCENY, THOUGH INTERESTINGLY ENOUGH, NOT FOR PROSTITUTION.

MAYBE HER CLIENTS DIDN'T WANT TO ADMIT HOW THEIR WALLETS ENDED UP IN SUCH CLOSE PROXIMITY TO MARY IN THE FIRST PLACE.

MARY DIDN'T ALLOW ANYONE TO DENY HER GENDER EXPRESSION. SHE SHOWED UP TO COURT IN WOMEN'S CLOTHES AND ENDURED LAUGHTER IN THE COURTROOM.

SOMEONE EVEN RIPPED HER WIG OFF BEFORE SHE WAS FOUND GUILTY OF GRAND LARCENY.

GUILTY!

BANG!

THE SENTENCE, FIVE YEARS AT SING SING PRISON,

PLACED HER AMONG THE MALE PRISONERS.

TO THIS DAY, NEARLY ALL INCARCERATED TRANSGENDER PEOPLE ARE PLACED BASED ON THE GENDER THEY WERE ASSIGNED AT BIRTH.

There is a ton of information online about this topic and prisons in general. Please refer to either of these websites for more information, further reading, and how to help prison reform organizations.

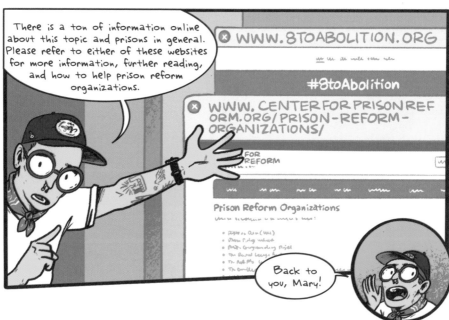

WWW.8TOABOLITION.ORG

#8toAbolition

WWW.CENTERFORPRISONREFORM.ORG/PRISON-REFORM-ORGANIZATIONS/

FOR REFORM

Prison Reform Organizations

Back to you, Mary!

MARY CONTINUED TO EXPERIENCE HARASSMENT AND TRANSPHOBIA FOR THE REST OF HER LIFE.

DURING HER TRIAL, ONE NEW YORK NEWSPAPER PRINTED AN ILLUSTRATION OF MARY WITH A CAPTION CALLING HER A "MAN MONSTER."

MAN-MONSTER SENTENCED TO FIVE YEARS AT SING SING

THE MAN MONSTER

ONCE OUT OF PRISON, MARY RETURNED TO SEX WORK AND CONTINUED TO WEAR THE CLOTHING ALIGNED WITH HER IDENTITY.

WHEN SHE WAS ARRESTED YET AGAIN FOR "CROSS-DRESSING," THE PRESS HAD A FIELD DAY WHEN SHE WAS FOUND IN POSSESSION OF:

A FAUX VAGINA, WHICH SHE HAD FASHIONED FOR HERSELF FROM COW STEAKS AND LEATHER.

MARY SURVIVED IN A WORLD THAT WAS HOSTILE TO BLACK TRANS SEX WORKERS.

NOT MUCH ELSE IS KNOWN ABOUT MARY AFTER HER SECOND ARREST.

flip!

MARY WAS RADICAL, FIERCE, AND FEARLESS, LIVING BOLDLY AS HERSELF UNDER IMPOSSIBLE CIRCUMSTANCES. I FIND HER SURVIVAL AMAZING.

LIVING OUTSIDE NORMS IS A CHALLENGE, ESPECIALLY WHEN THE VALUES YOU GREW UP WITH ARE AT ODDS WITH EVERYTHING YOU'RE FEELING ABOUT YOURSELF.

I DON'T TALK ABOUT IT OFTEN, BUT I TOO HAVE BEEN HURT, HARASSED, ASSAULTED, AND MISTREATED BECAUSE OF MY GENDER EXPRESSION AND QUEER SEXUALITY. THIS BIGOTRY TAKES A TOLL ON SOMEBODY, MENTALLY, PHYSICALLY, AND EMOTIONALLY.

SOME OF THESE MOMENTS STILL CUT SO DEEP THAT I'M NOT SURE HOW TO BEGIN TALKING ABOUT THEM.

BUT IT HELPS ME TO LEARN ABOUT PEOPLE WHO HAVE OVERCOME EVEN GREATER HARDSHIPS THAN I HAVE.

WHILE RESEARCHING QUEER PEOPLE IN THE HOLOCAUST, I CAME ACROSS ONE SUCH PERSON, A MAN NAMED MAGNUS HIRSCHFELD.

MAGNUS WAS ONE OF FEW GAY MEN THAT NEVER HAD TO HAVE FIRST-HAND CONTACT WITH THE NAZIS.

BUT THEIR BRUTAL REGIME STILL WREAKED HAVOC UPON HIS LIFE'S WORK.

BC 199

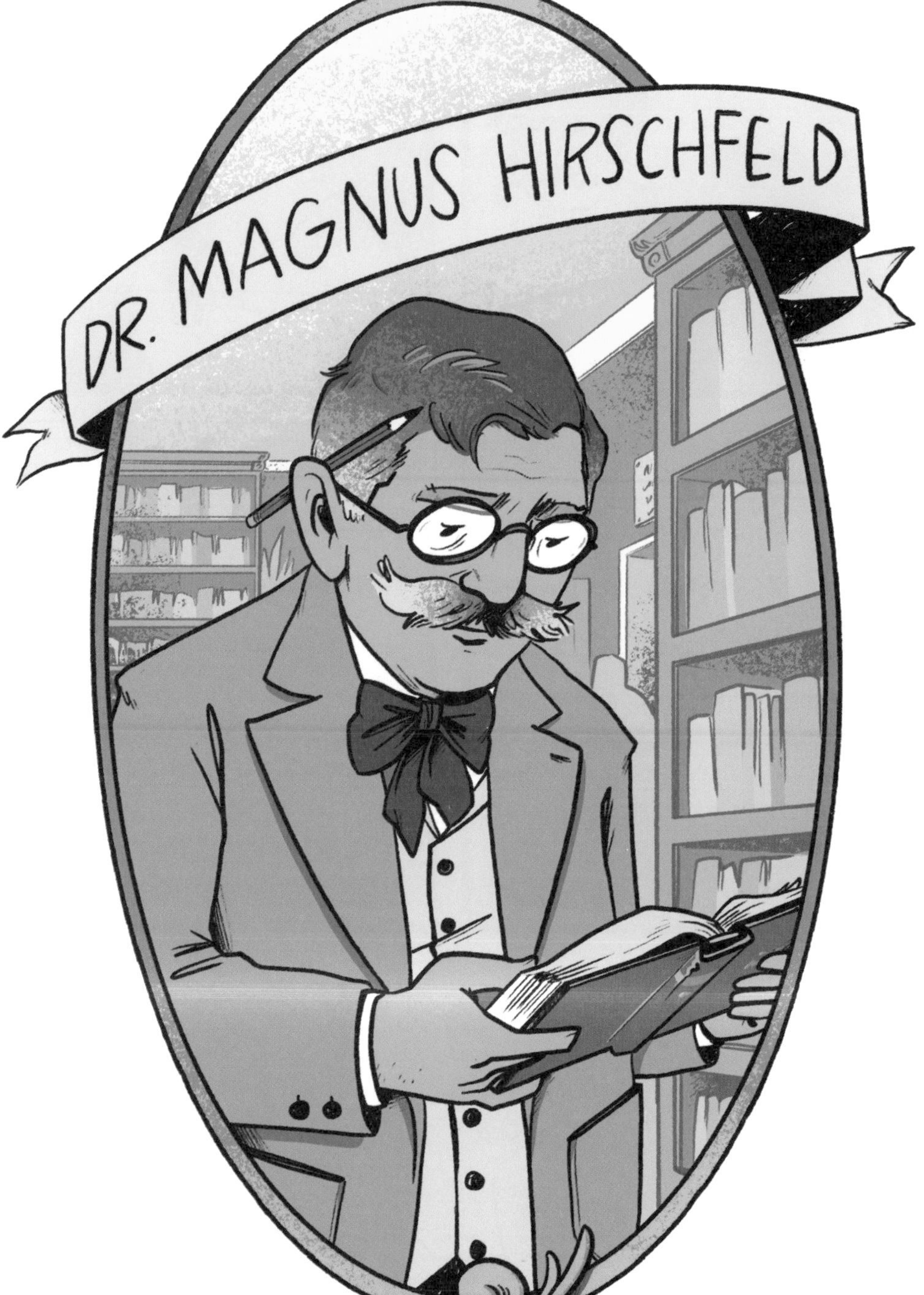
DR. MAGNUS HIRSCHFELD

MAGNUS HIRSCHFELD WAS BORN INTO A CONSERVATIVE ASHKENAZI JEWISH FAMILY IN KOLBERG, PRUSSIA, IN 1868.

HIS FATHER WAS A WELL-RESPECTED PHYSICIAN. HIS PUBLIC HEALTH EFFORTS WERE HIGHLY ESTEEMED IN KOLBERG.

AS A BOY, MAGNUS WAS FASCINATED BY HUMAN SEXUALITY AND OTHER BOYS.

HE WAS PARTICULARLY INTERESTED IN THE FACT THAT TWO PEOPLE OF THE SAME SEX COULD BE IN LOVE WITH EACHOTHER.

IN 1888, HE FOLLOWED IN HIS FATHER AND BOTH OF HIS BROTHERS' FOOTSTEPS BY BECOMING A MEDICAL STUDENT AT THE UNIVERSITY OF STRASBOURG.

BUT WHILE IN SCHOOL, MAGNUS WAS TRAUMATIZED BY A LECTURE ON "SEXUAL DEGENERACY."

HIS PROFESSOR TOLD A STORY OF A GAY MAN WHO WAS INCARCERATED IN AN ASYLUM FOR THIRTY YEARS FOR HIS SEXUAL PREFERENCE.

THEN, HE BROUGHT THE MAN FROM THE STORY OUT IN FRONT OF THE CLASS, FULLY NUDE, AND PARADED HIM AROUND LIKE A LAB RAT.

AS THE ROOM FILLED WITH LAUGHTER, MAGNUS WAS REVOLTED.

HE SEEMED TO BE THE ONLY ONE OF HIS CLASSMATES THAT SAW THIS AS UNFAIR TREATMENT.

Do you not think this is wrong?

PERHAPS THE GUILT HE FELT FOR NOT OPENLY OBJECTING TO WHAT HAPPENED IN CLASS PUSHED HIM TO EMBRACE AND LEARN EVERYTHING HE COULD ON HOMOSEXUALITY.

MAGNUS WROTE A PAMPHLET CAMPAIGNING FOR FAIR TREATMENT OF QUEER PEOPLE AND THE DECRIMINALIZATION OF GAY SEX.

AT THE TIME, SEX BETWEEN TWO MEMBERS OF THE SAME SEX WAS ILLEGAL IN GERMANY.

I urge you to read this!

THE SAME SPARK THAT INSPIRED MAGNUS TO DO HIS RESEARCH LIT HIM UPON A THRIVING GAY SCENE IN BERLIN.

HE FOUND A CHOSEN-FAMILY AND STARTED ASKING PEOPLE IN HIS CIRCLE TO TAKE SURVEYS ON SEX AND JOIN HIS CAMPAIGN TO REFORM GERMANY'S ANTI-GAY LAWS.

NOT EVERYONE WAS AS INTERESTED IN STARTING A REVOLUTION AS MAGNUS; SOME PEOPLE VIEWED HIM AS A TROUBLE MAKER.

IN 1895, FAMOUS POET AND PLAYWRIGHT OSCAR WILDE WAS ON TRIAL FOR INDECENCY AFTER HIS GAY AFFAIR WITH A BRITISH ARISTOCRAT BECAME PUBLIC.

You hear Wilde is going to court for a gay affair?

WHEN MAGNUS CAUGHT WIND OF THE NEWS, HE WAS OUTRAGED. THIS WAS NOT JUST A MATTER OF LOCAL MISTREATMENT, IT WAS HAPPENING AROUND THE WORLD!

WHAT!?

MAGNUS WORRIED HIS LONE EFFORTS WERE NOT ENOUGH TO CREATE REAL CHANGE, SO HE FOUNDED THE SCIENTIFIC HUMANITARIAN COMMITTEE, ONE OF THE WORLD'S EARLIEST QUEER ADVOCACY GROUPS.

JUSTICE THROUGH SCIENCE

THE COMMITTEE STUDIED SEXUALITY AND THEORIZED ABOUT GENDER.

MAGNUS COINED THE TERM "TRANSVESTITE," WHICH IS NOW OUT-DATED AND VIEWED AS OFFENSIVE. THE GROUP DISCUSSED THE IDEA OF A THIRD GENDER, AND LEARNED ABOUT THE LIVES OF INTERSEX PEOPLE.

MALE FEMALE

3RD GENDER = "INTERMEDIARY"

Okay, so you said you don't feel like a woman, nor do you feel like a man. What should we call this gender?

What about "intermediary"?

IN 1919, HE PURCHASED A VILLA IN BERLIN AND CONVERTED IT INTO THE INSTITUTE FOR SEXUAL SCIENCE, WHERE HIS TEAM FURTHERED THE RESEARCH AND MISSION THAT THE SCIENTIFIC HUMANITARIAN COMMITTEE HAD ORIGINALLY SET FORTH.

MAGNUS BEGAN WORKING WITH A SURGEON FROM VIENNA NAMED EUGEN STEINACH. THE PAIR DEVELOPED EARLY TECHNIQUES FOR GENDER-AFFIRMATION OR GENDER-ALIGNMENT SURGERIES.

Gender-affirmation surgeries don't change someone's gender, rather they change the body in which one experiences their gender.

SOME PEOPLE CHOOSE SURGERY TO ALLEVIATE FEELINGS OF DYSPHORIA, OR TO ALIGN THEIR BODY AND MIND.

WHILE SOME MIGHT NOT CHOOSE SURGERY, IT IS A COMPLETELY PERSONAL CHOICE.

Dysphoria may be difficult to understand if you do not experience it.

An example of it would be me, in a coffee shop, being called "she," "her," or "ma'am."

I was assigned female at birth, but I don't identify as such, and it feels wrong to be seen as a girl.

MAGNUS AND HIS TEAM SPENT MANY YEARS PERFORMING VARIOUS SURGERIES THAT WERE NEVER FULLY REALIZED UNTIL 1922, WHEN DORA RICHTER CAME ALONG.

Dora, time to get up.

THE TEAM AND DR. FELIX ABRAHAM HAD COMPLETED A SUCCESSFUL MALE TO FEMALE AFFIRMATION SURGERY ON DORA.

Are we finally done?

IF YOU'VE EVER SEEN THE FILM, **THE DANISH GIRL**, YOU MIGHT KNOW MAGNUS'S NEXT CLIENT.

OVER TWO YEARS, MAGNUS AND HIS MEDICAL TEAM PERFORMED FIVE AFFIRMATION SURGERIES ON DANISH ARTIST LILI ELBE. NUMEROUS PAPERS RAN STORIES ON HER IN DENMARK AND GERMANY.

ADVANCED SURGERY

LILI DIED AFTER A SURGERY IN 1931. A FAILED ATTEMPT TO ENABLE HER TO CARRY A CHILD.

LILI ELBE

MAGNUS AND HIS FELLOW SURGEONS WERE NOT THE ONLY PEOPLE WHO WORKED AT THE INSTITUTE.

DORA RICHTER WORKED THERE AS A MAID. TO PREVENT THE POLICE FROM ARRESTING HER FOR "CROSS-DRESSING," MAGNUS GOT GOVERNMENT PROTECTION FOR DORA TO WEAR WOMEN'S CLOTHING TO WORK.

MAGNUS'S TWO LIFE-PARTNERS, KARL GIESE AND LI SHIU TONG, WORKED THERE, TOO. TODAY, THEY MIGHT BE CALLED POLYAMOROUS, IN WHICH EACH PARTNER IN A RELATIONSHIP CONSENSUALLY DATES OTHER PEOPLE.

KARL GIESE WAS THE HEAD OF THE ARCHIVES DEPARTMENT, TAKING CARE OF THE EXTENSIVE COLLECTION OF OVER 20,000 VOLUMES AND 35,000 PHOTOS OF SEXUAL AND MEDICAL RESEARCH DOCUMENTS.

AND LI SHIU TONG WAS MAGNUS'S PROTÉGÉ, TRAVEL COMPANION, AND TRANSLATOR.

AS ADOLF HITLER CAME INTO POWER IN GERMANY, SO BEGAN THE DEMISE OF MAGNUS'S WORK.

IN 1933, THE NAZIS RANSACKED THE INSTITUTE, SETTING AFLAME MOST OF ITS ARCHIVES.

THEY KEPT DOCUMENTS NAMING THOSE THAT OBTAINED SEXUAL COUNSELING, SURGERIES, AND HORMONE THERAPY AT THE INSTITUTE. HITLER ADDED THESE PEOPLE TO HIS "PINK LISTS," WHICH WERE REGISTERS OF GAY AND TRANSGENDER TARGETS FOR NAZI RAIDS.

MAGNUS FLED TO FRANCE, WHERE HE TRIED TO REOPEN HIS FACILITIES.

BUT SHORTLY AFTER MOVING TO FRANCE, MAGNUS DIED AT THE AGE OF 67 FROM A HEART ATTACK.

THREE YEARS LATER, KARL DIED BY SUICIDE WHILE ON THE RUN FROM THE NAZIS.

HIER WOHNTE
KARL GIESE
JG. 1898
FLUCHT 1938
FRANKREIGH
TSCHEGHOSLOWAKEI
FLUCHT IN DEN TOO
16. 3. 1938
BRNO

LI WENT HOME TO HONG KONG BEFORE MOVING THE REMAINS OF MAGNUS'S ARCHIVE TO VANCOUVER, WHERE HE DIED. NOT MUCH IS KNOWN ABOUT LI'S LIFE IN CANADA. HIS FAMILY DISOWNED HIM.

李兆堂
SHIU TONG LI
1907 - 1993

WHILE MOST OF MAGNUS'S WORK WAS DESTROYED, A FEW BITS AND PIECES REMAIN.

A GAY DRAMA FILM WRITTEN AND PRODUCED BY MAGNUS, **DIFFERENT FROM THE OTHERS**, WAS LOST FOR DECADES. IT WAS RECENTLY RESTORED BY THE UCLA FILM & TELEVISION ARCHIVE.

SOME OF HIS BOOKS SURVIVED THE NAZI'S WRATH, LIKE **BERLIN'S THIRD SEX**, WHICH DOCUMENTS THE BERLIN LGBTQ+ SCENE FROM MAGNUS'S PERSPECTIVE AS AN INSIDER.

MAGNUS AND HIS TEAM PAVED THE WAY FOR GENDER-AFFIRMING SURGERIES AND HORMONE THERAPY.

THE MAGNUS HIRSCHFELD SOCIETY STILL EXISTS TODAY IN GERMANY, WORKING TO COLLECT MISSING PIECES FROM MAGNUS'S LIFE.

DECADES LATER, HEALTH INSURANCE COMPANIES STILL REFUSE TO COVER TRANSITION-RELATED CARE LIKE THERAPY, HORMONES, AND SURGERIES.

NOT TO MENTION THAT SOME DOCTORS STILL REFUSE TO PROVIDE CARE TO TRANSGENDER PATIENTS,

WHETHER IT'S RELATED TO TRANSITIONAL CARE OR NOT.

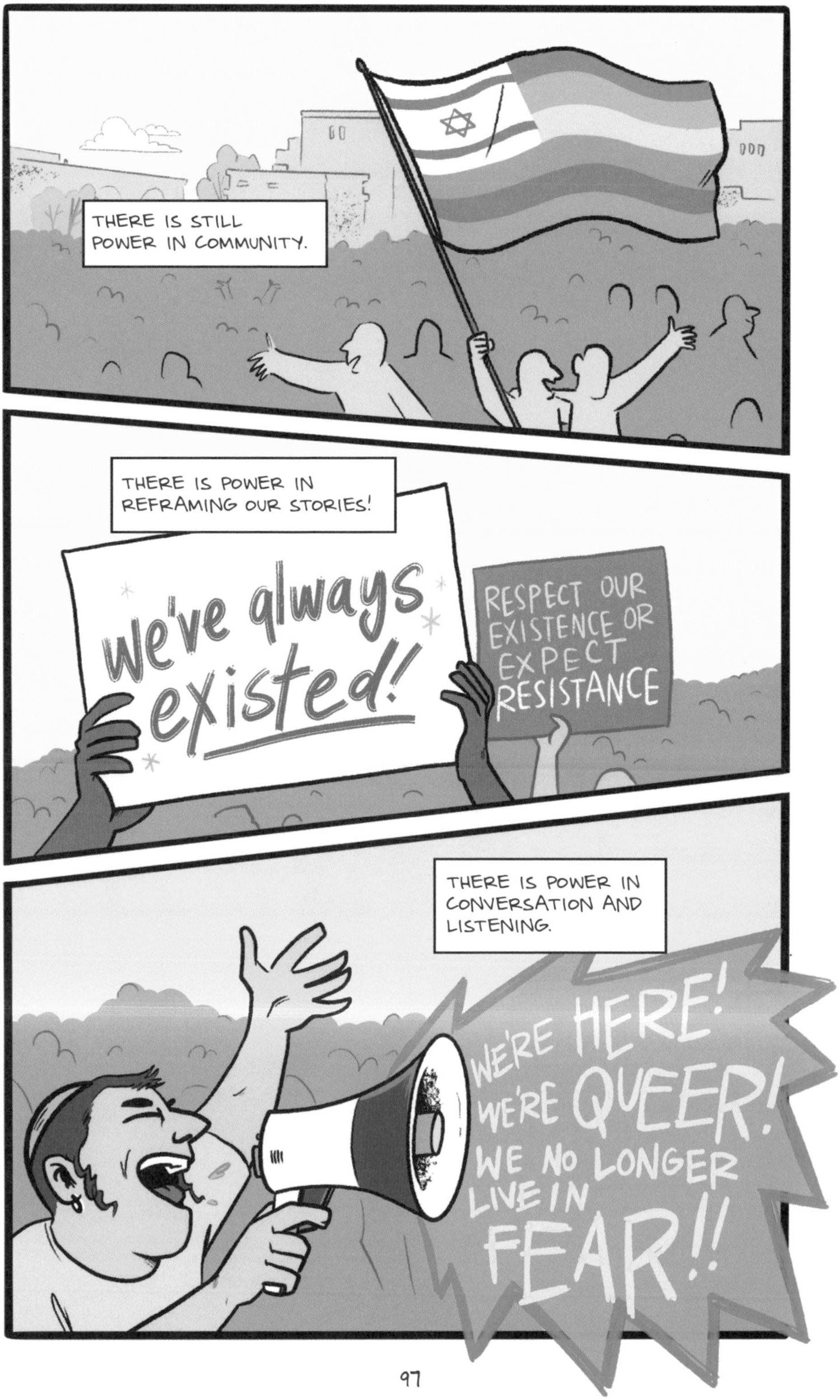
THERE IS STILL POWER IN COMMUNITY.
THERE IS POWER IN REFRAMING OUR STORIES!
we've always existed!
RESPECT OUR EXISTENCE OR EXPECT RESISTANCE
THERE IS POWER IN CONVERSATION AND LISTENING.
WE'RE HERE! WE'RE QUEER! WE NO LONGER LIVE IN FEAR!!

IGNORANCE KEEPS HISTORY STAGNANT AND REPEATABLE.

THE SECTION OF THE GERMAN CRIMINAL CODE THAT SPARKED MAGNUS'S ACTIVISM WAS FINALLY ABOLISHED IN 1994. THIS MORE THAN 100-YEAR-OLD MANDATE STATED THAT "UNNATURAL SEXUAL OFFENSES" BETWEEN MEN WERE PUNISHABLE BY UP TO SIX MONTHS IN PRISON.

I HOPE MAGNUS WOULD BE PROUD OF THE PROGRESS HE INSPIRED.

BECAUSE OF PIONEERS IN SEXUAL STUDIES LIKE MAGNUS, MY FRIENDS IN THE UNITED STATES HAVE BEEN ABLE TO ACCESS GENDER-AFFIRMING SURGERY.

MAGNUS PERFORMED SURGERIES FROM THE LATE 1920s UP UNTIL THE 1950s. AT THE TIME, PHYSICIANS PERFORMED THESE SURGERIES RARELY, AND MOSTLY IN EUROPE.

IN MY RESEARCH ON THE HISTORY OF SURGERY, I LEARNED ABOUT TWO WOMEN FROM THE UNITED STATES WHO HOPED TO TRAVEL TO EUROPE TO TRANSITION; CHRISTINE JORGENSON, WHO WAS WELL KNOWN IN AMERICAN MEDIA, AND A WOMAN SHE INSPIRED, CARLETT BROWN.

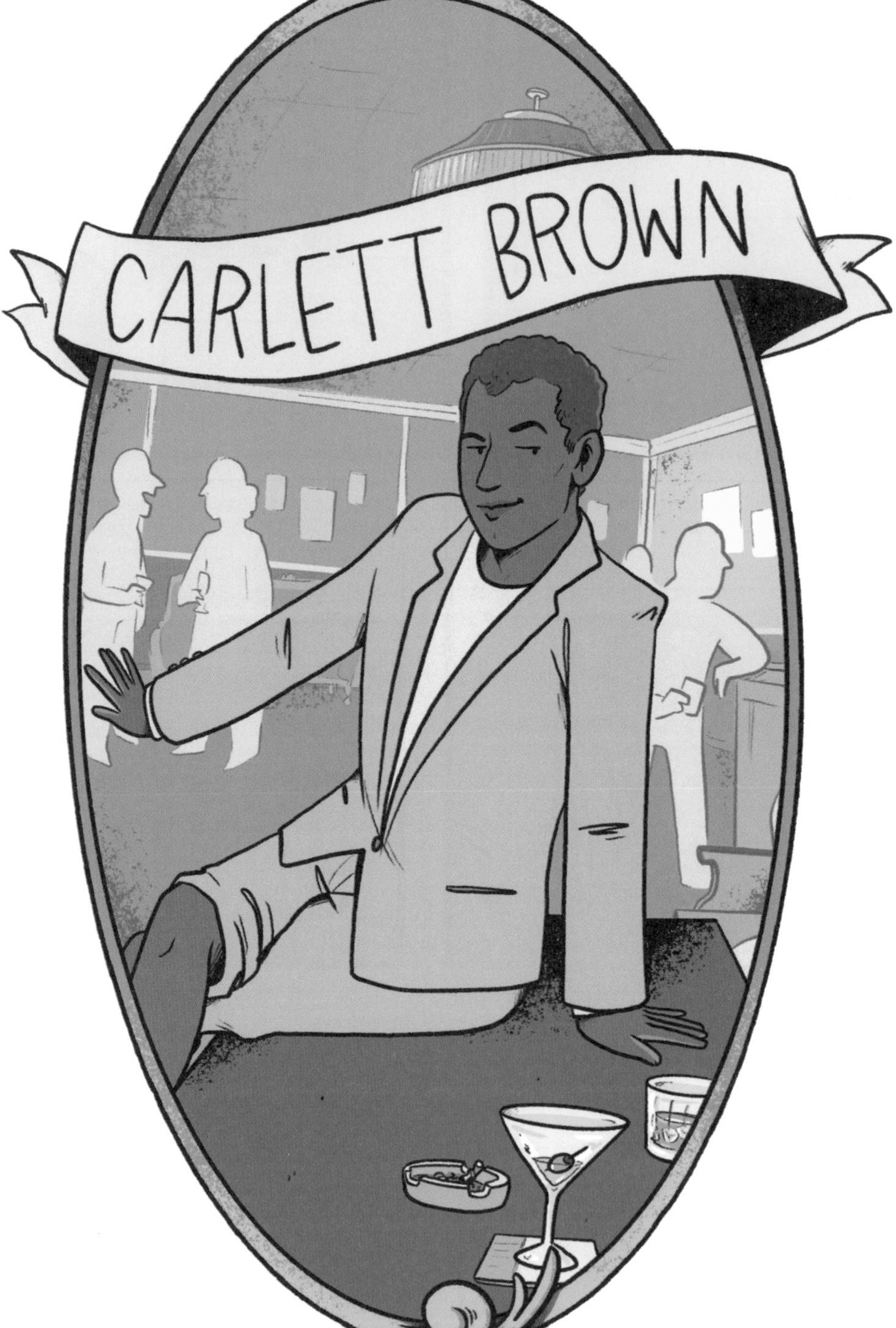
CARLETT BROWN

LIKE MARY JONES, MANY DETAILS OF CARLETT'S LIFE WERE NOT RECORDED.

CARLETT WAS ASSIGNED MALE AT BIRTH IN 1927.

IN ORDER TO ACCESS MUCH-NEEDED MEDICAL CARE, CARLETT JOINED THE U.S. NAVY AT THE AGE OF 23 DURING THE KOREAN WAR.

TODAY, MANY PEOPLE CONTINUE TO ENLIST IN THE MILITARY TO AFFORD HEALTHCARE IN AMERICA.

G.I. MEDICAL

CARLETT HAD REGULAR NOSEBLEEDS AND RECTAL BLEEDING THAT OCCURRED THREE DAYS A MONTH.

HER DOCTOR FOUND THAT GLANDS TYPICAL OF THE UTERINE SYSTEM WERE CAUSING HER TO "MENSTRUATE," AND SUGGESTED SURGERY TO REMOVE THEM.

We need to remove the female glands.

BUT CARLETT REFUSED. SHE FELT THE GLANDS AFFIRMED SOMETHING SHE HAD KNOWN ALL ALONG:

SHE WAS A WOMAN.

I've got some medical facts for ya!

Remember when I said Magnus researched intersex people?

Well, Carlett was born intersex.

CARLETT → MAGNUS

Intersex is an umbrella term for a wide range of sex traits or reproductive anatomy.

IN AMERICA, WHERE WE ADHERE STRICTLY TO A TWO GENDER, MALE/FEMALE BINARY,

M   F

PARENTS OFTEN ELECT FOR THEIR INTERSEX CHILDREN TO UNDERGO INVASIVE SURGERY, CHOOSING TO RAISE THEM AS EITHER MALE OR FEMALE.

THERE IS NO ONE SINGULAR INTERSEX EXPERIENCE. FOR INSTANCE, SOME INTERSEX PEOPLE DON'T IDENTIFY WITH THE TRANS OR QUEER COMMUNITY.

But changing a child's body without consent is vile.

INTERSEX PEOPLE ARE AS COMMON AS RED-HEADS

In 2013, the United Nations stated these nonconsensual surgeries are a violation. of human rights.

If you'd like some more info...

⊗ INTERACTADVOCATES.ORG

interACT

What is intersex?

CARLETT ONLY SPENT SIX MONTHS IN THE NAVY. SHE WAS DISCHARGED FOR "SERIOUS MENTAL ILLNESS" AND "WANTING TO BE A WOMAN."

AFTER THE MILITARY, CARLETT WAS WILLING TO GO TO THE ENDS OF THE EARTH TO TRANSITION.

SHE SPENT AS MUCH TIME AS SHE COULD FINDING INFORMATION ON HOW TO TRANSITION AND PASS AS A WOMAN.

IN THE MEANTIME, SHE WORKED AS A SHAKE DANCER IN BARS FOR MONEY AND SOLD PLASMA.

CARLETT READ ABOUT CHRISTINE JORGENSEN, WHO WAS IN THE LOCAL PAPER FOR RECEIVING GENDER-AFFIRMING SURGERIES.

CHRISTINE HAD ALSO SERVED IN THE MILITARY. SHE WAS DRAFTED INTO THE AMERICAN ARMY DURING WORLD WAR II.

WHEN SHE GOT OUT OF THE SERVICE, SHE WORKED, WENT TO SCHOOL, AND TRAVELED TO COPENHAGEN, WHERE SHE LEARNED ABOUT GENDER-AFFIRMING SURGERY.

THE NEWS OF CHRISTINE IN THE PRESS MADE HER FAMOUS, AND CARLETT'S FIRE WAS LIT.

BY 1952 SHE WAS SCHEDULED TO UNDERGO OPERATIONS FROM CHRISTINE'S DOCTOR.

MEANWHILE, CARLETT HAD LONG BEEN COURTING A ROMANTIC CONNECTION WITH U.S. ARMY SARGENT EUGENE MARTIN, WHO WAS STATIONED IN GERMANY.

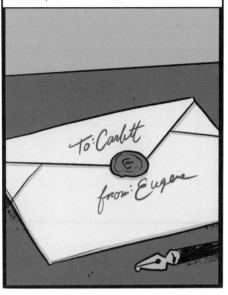

PERHAPS CARLETT ALSO HAD HER EYE TRAINED ON MARRYING EUGENE,

AND KNEW IT MAY BE A LEGAL IMPOSSIBILITY IF SHE DIDN'T PASS IN PUBLIC AS A WOMAN.

I just want to become a woman as quickly as possible, that's all.

I'll become a citizen of any country that will allow me the treatment that I need.

TURNS OUT, CHRISTINE MADE THE PROCESS LOOK INCREDIBLY EASY ON PAPER.

IT WASN'T.

CARLETT GOT A TRAVEL PASSPORT AND MADE PLANS TO MEET WITH DR. HAMBURGER IN COPENHAGEN IN AUGUST OF 1953.

ONCE IN COPENHAGEN, DR. HAMBURGER TOLD CARLETT SHE NEEDED TO BE A DANISH CITIZEN IN ORDER TO RECEIVE HIS SURGICAL CARE, SO SHE RETURNED TO BOSTON TO RENOUNCE HER U.S. CITIZENSHIP.

THE LONG WAITING PROCESS IN THE U.S. FOR DANISH CITIZENSHIP TOOK A FEW TURNS.

IN AMERICA, CROSS-DRESSING WAS STILL AN ARRESTABLE OFFENSE. ONE NIGHT, CARLETT WAS ARRESTED FOR WEARING WOMEN'S CLOTHING AND JAILED UNTIL MORNING.

CLINK!

AS SOON AS SHE GOT OUT, THE U.S. GOVERNMENT TOLD HER SHE COULDN'T RENOUNCE CITIZENSHIP UNTIL SHE PAID $1,200 IN BACK TAXES.

PRECINT 169

SHE COULDN'T AFFORD THE TAXES, SO SHE WENT BACK TO WORK AND POSTPONED HER EURO-TRIP.

A DISTANT COUSIN HELPED HER GET A JOB WORKING AS A CHEF IN AN IOWA STATE FRATERNITY HOUSE FOR $60 A WEEK.

IOWA STATE UNIVERSITY

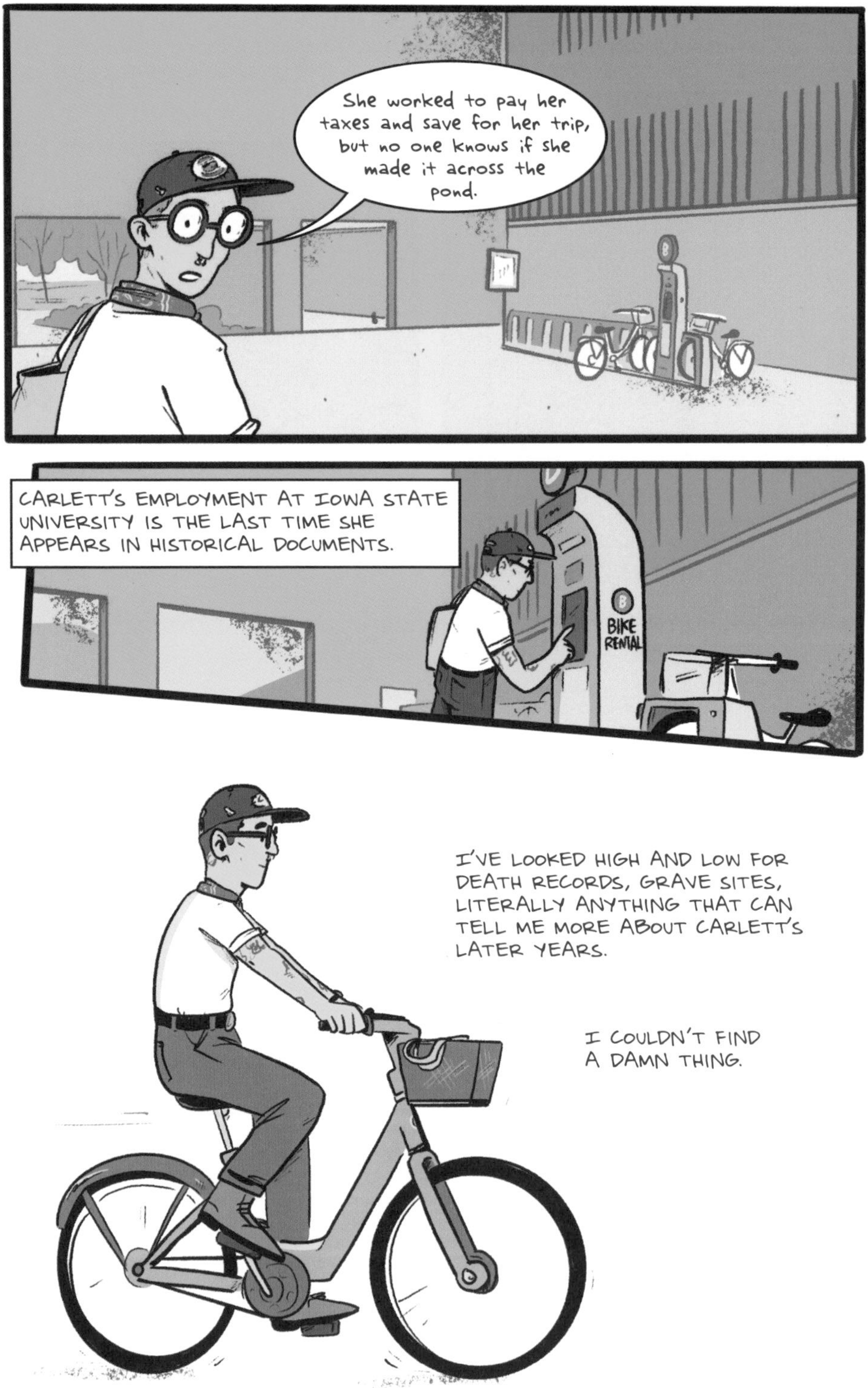
She worked to pay her taxes and save for her trip, but no one knows if she made it across the pond.
CARLETT'S EMPLOYMENT AT IOWA STATE UNIVERSITY IS THE LAST TIME SHE APPEARS IN HISTORICAL DOCUMENTS.
BIKE RENTAL
I'VE LOOKED HIGH AND LOW FOR DEATH RECORDS, GRAVE SITES, LITERALLY ANYTHING THAT CAN TELL ME MORE ABOUT CARLETT'S LATER YEARS.
I COULDN'T FIND A DAMN THING.

TO ME, CARLETT IS FOREVER A TRANSGENDER LEGEND.

I HOPE THAT SHE MADE IT TO DENMARK AND GOT HER SURGERIES,

AND THAT SHE WAS ABLE TO MARRY THE MAN OF HER DREAMS.

Oh, hey, friends, long time no see. What y'all up to?

Hey, Shelby!

We're educating people about San Antonio civil rights history. The Woolworth building behind us is the first place in San Antonio to have a desegregated lunch counter.

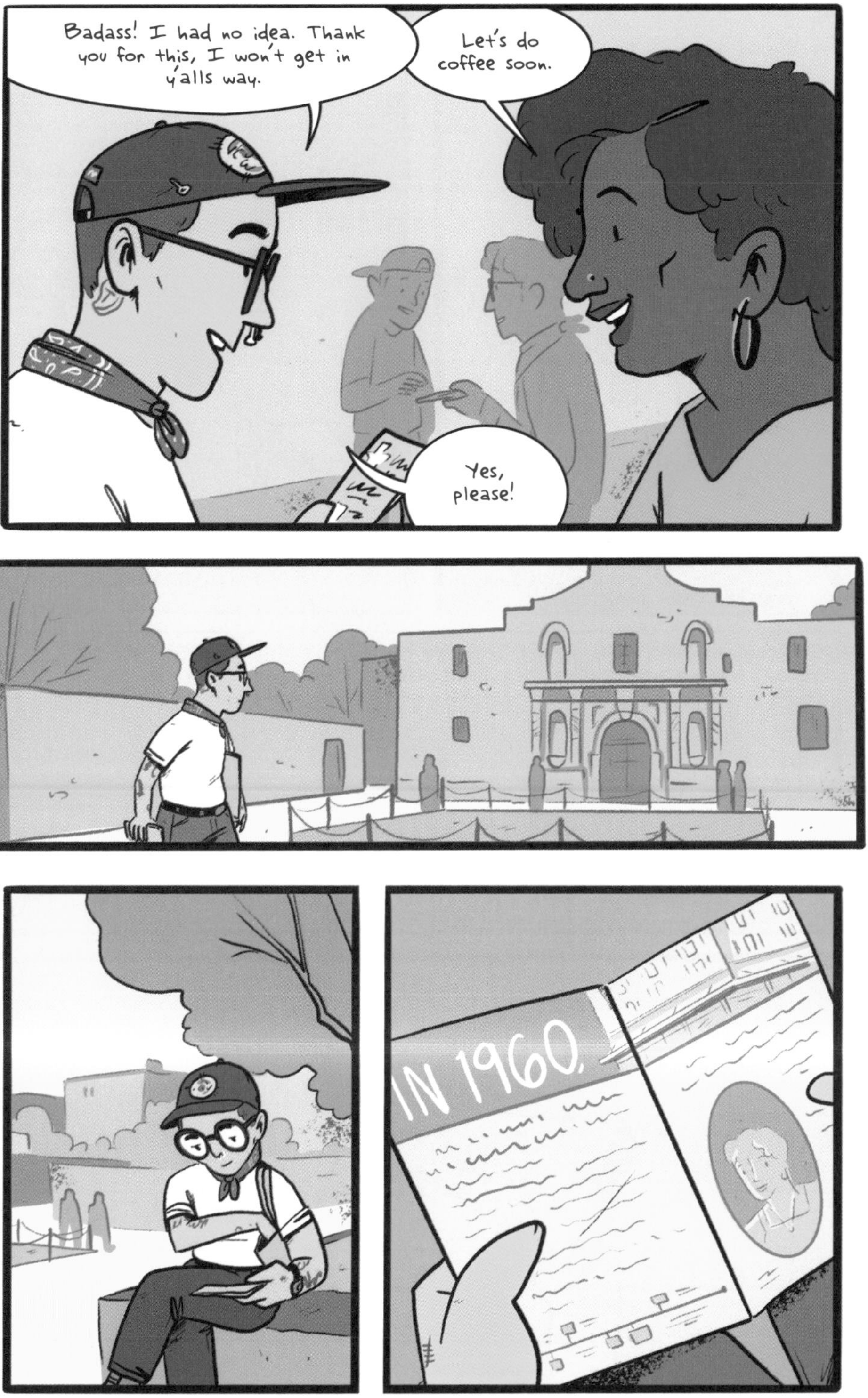
Badass! I had no idea. Thank you for this, I won't get in y'alls way.
Let's do coffee soon.
Yes, please!
IN 1960.

Oh, I never finished that Pauli drawing...

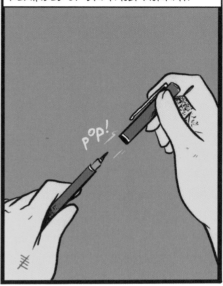

WHENEVER I THINK OF THE CIVIL RIGHTS MOVEMENT IN THE 1960s, I'M REMINDED OF DR. PAULI MURRAY.

POP!

I OFTEN WONDER HOW PEOPLE USED TO EXPLORE THEIR GENDER IDENTITY BEFORE WE HAD THE VAST TERMINOLOGY WE DO TODAY.

DR. PAULI MURRAY *

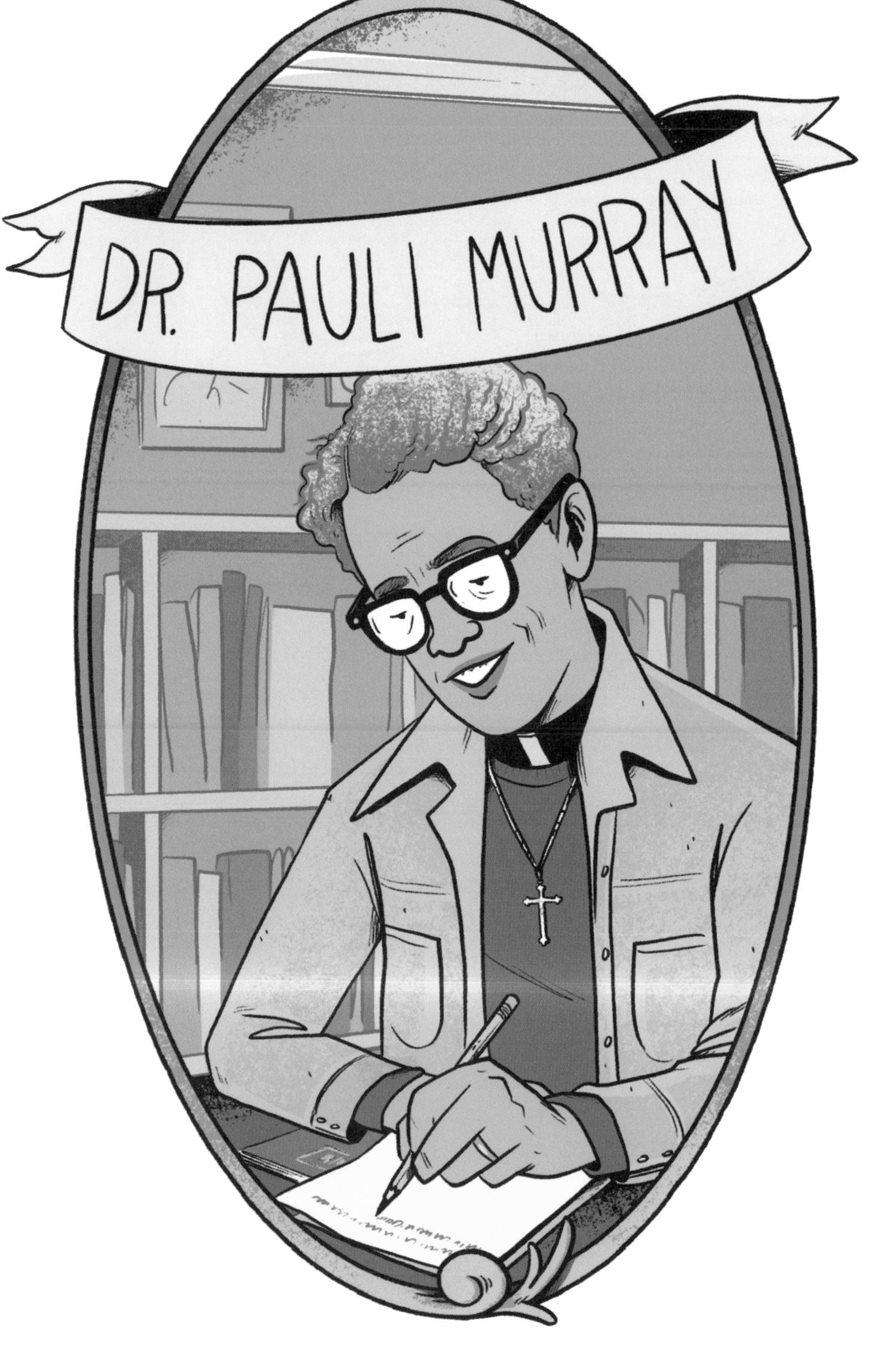
DR. PAULI MURRAY

PAULI WAS ASSIGNED FEMALE AT BIRTH IN A MIXED-RACE FAMILY IN 1910 IN BALTIMORE, MARYLAND.

PAULI WAS ESSENTIALLY ORPHANED AT THE AGE OF FOUR WHEN THEIR MOTHER SUDDENLY DIED OF A CEREBRAL HEMORRHAGE. THEIR FATHER COULD NOT TAKE CARE OF ALL SIX CHILDREN ALONE, SO PAULI WENT TO LIVE WITH GRANDPARENTS IN NORTH CAROLINA.

MOST OF THE WOMEN IN PAULI'S LIFE WERE TEACHERS, SO IT WAS ONLY NATURAL THAT PAULI WANTED TO ADVANCE THEIR EDUCATION.

AFTER HIGH SCHOOL, PAULI MARRIED A MAN NAMED ROY "BILLY" WYNN IN SECRET.

THE COUPLE ONLY SPENT A FEW MONTHS TOGETHER BEFORE SEPARATING. PAULI LATER WROTE THAT THE SECRET MARRIAGE WAS A REGRETTABLE DISASTER.

AS THE GREAT DEPRESSION SET IN, JOBS WERE SCARCE. PAULI TOOK A GIG SELLING SUBSCRIPTIONS TO AN ACADEMIC JOURNAL THAT BELONGED TO A CIVIL RIGHTS ORGANIZATION IN NEW YORK CITY.

PAULI RESIGNED DUE TO POOR HEALTH AND ENDED UP TAKING A POSITION AT A C.C.C. CAMP FOR UNEMPLOYED WOMEN, WHERE THEY MET FIRST LADY ELEANOR ROOSEVELT.

THIS IS ALSO AROUND THE TIME THAT PAULI BEGAN TO QUESTION THEIR GENDER.

IN 1931, PAULI CHANGED THEIR BIRTH NAME AND BEGAN PURSUING GENDER AFFIRMING TREATMENTS LIKE HORMONE THERAPY.

The Imp!
1931

HORMONE THERAPY, FOR TRANSGENDER OR NONBINARY PATIENTS, IS A TREATMENT PROCESS TO ALIGN ONE'S SECONDARY SEXUAL CHARACTERISTICS WITH ONE'S GENDER IDENTITY.

THIS TYPICALLY INVOLVES EITHER ESTROGEN OR TESTOSTERONE INJECTIONS.

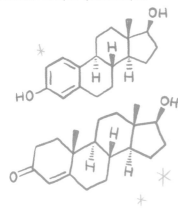

IN PAULI'S LIFETIME, HORMONE THERAPY WAS USUALLY ONLY ADMINISTERED TO PEOPLE WITH SPECIFIC MEDICAL AILMENTS LIKE CANCER. PAULI, LIKE MANY OF DR. MAGNUS HIRSCHFELD'S PATIENTS, WAS DENIED TESTOSTERONE.

There is absolutely no way that I could do that for you.

AROUND THIS SAME PERIOD, PAULI BEGAN TO GET INVOLVED IN CIVIL RIGHTS WORK.

THEY WROTE ARTICLES AND WERE INVOLVED IN SIT-IN PROTESTS.

PAULI CAMPAIGNED TO BE ADMITTED TO AN ALL-WHITE GRADUATE SCHOOL, THE UNIVERSITY OF NORTH CAROLINA.

AND WAS DENIED.

Those bastards...

PAULI'S CAMPAIGN GOT NATIONAL ATTENTION AND WAS BACKED BY ELEANOR ROOSEVELT.

PAULI HAD AN INTENSE HUNGER FOR JUSTICE AND EDUCATION.

ahem

Hope is a crushed stalk
Between clenched fingers

Hope is a bird's wing
Broken by a stone

PAULI ENDED UP AT HOWARD UNIVERSITY AND LATER GRADUATED AS VALEDICTORIAN WITH A LAW DEGREE. WHILE THERE, THEY FELT OPPRESSION FROM NOT BEING WHITE OR MALE.

THEY COINED THE TREATMENT THEY HAD TO ENDURE, "JANE CROW," A PLAY ON THE JIM CROW LAWS THAT ENFORCED RACIAL SEGREGATION IN THE U.S. AFTER THE ABOLITION OF SLAVERY.

AS THE CIVIL RIGHTS MOVEMENT GAINED MOMENTUM, PAULI MOVED BACK TO NEW YORK.

IN 1951, PAULI WROTE A BOOK, **STATES LAWS ON RACE AND COLOR**. THURGOOD MARSHALL, HEAD OF THE N.A.A.C.P.'S LEGAL DEPARTMENT AND LATER SUPREME COURT JUSTICE, CALLED THIS WORK...

...a Bible for civil rights litigators.

WHEN THURGOOD WAS CRAFTING HIS LEGAL STRATEGY FOR THE BROWN V. BOARD OF EDUCATION CASE IN 1954, WHICH DESEGREGATED AMERICAN PUBLIC SCHOOLS, HE USED KEY POINTS FROM PAULI'S WRITING.

BUT THURGOOD MARSHALL WAS BEING TARGETED BY SENATOR JOSEPH McCARTHY AT THE TIME, WHOSE VICIOUS CAMPAIGN TO...

Protect the U.S. from communism...

WAS TO USED SILENCE ACTIVISTS, POLITICIANS, AND ANYONE WORKING FOR CIVIL RIGHTS.

PAULI FELT THE WEIGHT OF McCARTHYISM IN 1952 WHEN THEY APPLIED FOR A JOB AT THE STATE DEPARTMENT-THEIR REFERENCES, ELEANOR ROOSEVELT, A. PHILLIP RANDOLPH, AND THURGOOD MARSHALL, WERE CONSIDERED TOO RADICAL AND PAULI WAS DENIED THE JOB.

ELEANOR ROOSEVELT

THURGOOD MARSHALL

A. PHILLIP RANDOLPH

TRIP!

PAULI TOOK A JOB AT A NEW LAW FIRM, WHERE THEY MET THEIR PARTNER OF THE NEXT FIFTEEN YEARS, IRENE.

IN 1960, PAULI WENT TO GHANA TO EXPLORE THEIR AFRICAN ROOTS AND TEACH LAW.

THEN PAULI RETURNED TO AMERICA TO ENROLL AT YALE LAW SCHOOL TO EARN A DOCTORATE.

IN 1961, PRESIDENT J.F.K. APPOINTED PAULI TO THE COMMITTEE ON CIVIL AND POLITICAL RIGHTS, WHERE THEY WORKED CLOSELY WITH PEOPLE LIKE MARTIN LUTHER KING JR.

PAULI WAS CRITICAL OF THE WAY MEN DOMINATED CIVIL RIGHTS LEADERSHIP,

AND FOUNDED THE NATIONAL ORGANIZATION FOR WOMEN (**N.O.W.**) IN 1966, ALONG WITH BETTY FRIEDAN AND OTHERS.

ALTHOUGH PAULI HELPED FOUND **N.O.W.**, THE ORGANIZATION DIDN'T PROPERLY ADDRESS ISSUES SPECIFIC TO BLACK AND WORKING-CLASS WOMEN.

SO PAULI LEFT.

FROM THE 1920S UNTIL ABOUT THE 1970S, PAULI NOTICED A CULTURE OF "RESPECTABILITY POLITICS" IN THE CIVIL RIGHTS MOVEMENT.

PEOPLE ONLY SEEMED TO TAKE SERIOUSLY THOSE THAT WERE EDUCATED, HETEROSEXUAL, MARRIED, PEACEFUL, NON-RADICAL, AND CHRISTIAN AS LEADERS.

PERHAPS THIS IS ONE OF THE REASONS PAULI SPENT MUCH OF THEIR LIFE IN A RELATIONSHIP WITH A WOMAN AND RECORDED INTIMATE THOUGHTS, BUT NEVER CAME OUT IN PUBLIC AS ALIGNED WITH A SEXUAL PREFERENCE.

YEARS LATER, AFTER IRENE DIED, PAULI BECAME A CANDIDATE FOR ORDINATION AT GENERAL THEOLOGICAL SEMINARY.

IN THE 1970S, THE CHURCH STARTED BREAKING TRADITION, ALLOWING NOT JUST WHITE MEN TO BE PRIESTS. PAULI BECAME ONE OF THE FIRST BLACK PEOPLE IN AMERICA TO BECOME AN ORDAINED EPISCOPAL PRIEST.

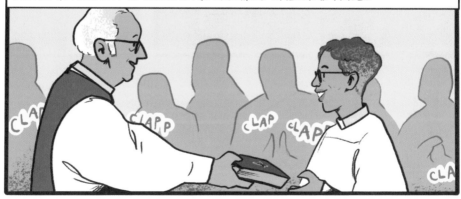

PAULI CONTINUED MINISTRY WORK UNTIL THEY DIED OF PANCREATIC CANCER IN JULY OF 1985.

THEY ARE BURIED UNDER THE SAME HEADSTONE AS IRENE.

TODAY, PAULI MURRAY IS CONSIDERED A HOLY PERSON BY THE EPISCOPAL CHURCH, AND THEIR LEGACY IS CELEBRATED EVERY JULY 1st WITH A CEREMONIAL FEAST.

THE U.S. DEPARTMENT OF THE INTERIOR ALSO DESIGNATED PAULI'S CHILDHOOD HOME IN NORTH CAROLINA A NATIONAL LANDMARK.

PAULI'S LEGACY TEACHES US TO BE CONSCIOUS OF INTERSECTIONALITY.

EACH OF US IS DEALT A DIFFERENT HAND, AND WE SHOULD BE ABLE TO STEP BACK AND SEE HOW WE BENEFIT OR ARE HINDERED BY OUR RACE, GENDER, SEXUALITY, RELIGION, CLASS, AND PHYSICAL AND MENTAL CAPABILITIES.

THINK OF IT THIS WAY: YOU WOULDN'T JUST CONNECT ONE SECTION OF A PUZZLE AND CALL IT DONE.

YOU WOULD FINISH THE CORNERS, MIDDLE, AND EDGES UNTIL THE WHOLE PICTURE COMES INTO VIEW.

PAULI KEPT ASPECTS OF THEIR GENDER AND SEXUALITY PRIVATE.

I THINK A LOT OF US RETREAT INTO OUR RESPECTIVE CLOSETS FROM TIME TO TIME FOR SELF-PRESERVATION.

WHEN YOU LIVE IN A PLACE THAT DOESN'T ACCEPT YOUR "LIFESTYLE," AND WHEN A LOT OF YOUR FAMILY DOESN'T EITHER, GOING BACK INTO THE CLOSET FROM TIME TO TIME IS INEVITABLE.

BUT ALL OF THE TIMES I'VE DONE IT FOR SAFETY HAVE ONLY MADE MY LIFE OUTSIDE OF THE CLOSET FEEL MORE FULFILLING.

I OFTEN WONDER WHAT IT WOULD'VE BEEN LIKE GROWING UP IN A CHURCH ACCEPTING OF QUEER AND TRANS IDENTITIES.

WHAT IF I HAD A QUEER AND/OR GENDER-VARIANT MINISTER LIKE PAULI MURRAY? WOULD I HAVE STRUGGLED WITH GOD AS A TEENAGER AS MUCH AS I DID?

IN COLLEGE, MY CHRISTIAN FRIENDS AND I COULDN'T FIND A CHURCH THAT ACCEPTED LGBTQ+ PEOPLE.

I feel like the preacher avoided all of our questions.

Yeah, he just circled the conversation around and didn't answer anything. How do you feel, Shelby?

I'm not going back there.

WHEN I CAME OUT AS NONBINARY ON FACEBOOK, ONE OF THE LEADERS OF MY CHURCH HARASSED ME ONLINE.

GOD HAS A PLAN FOR YOU

I IMAGINE I WOULD HAVE HAD A MUCH MORE POSITIVE EXPERIENCE WITH MY GENDER AND SEXUALITY IF MY CHURCH WAS ACCEPTING.

I DON'T HAVE A PROBLEM WITH SPIRITUALITY ITSELF,

I BELIEVE IT'S A BEAUTIFUL WAY TO MAKE SENSE OF THIS WEIRD AND PAINFUL WORLD.

IT DID A LOT OF GOOD FOR MY FATHER WHEN HE WAS BATTLING CANCER, AND I THINK IT HELPED HIM MAKE PEACE WITH DEATH.

I'm outside when ur ready.

BUT THERE WAS A PERIOD OF TIME WHERE I FOLLOWED A RELIGION THAT DIDN'T WANT ME.

I USED TO STAY UP LATE AT NIGHT, FIGHTING GOD IN MY PRAYERS, ASKING OVER AND OVER WHY I FELT SO STRONGLY ABOUT BEING TOLD IT'S WRONG TO BE QUEER.

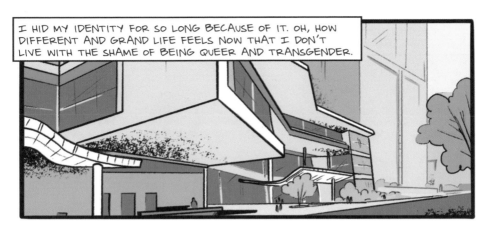

I HID MY IDENTITY FOR SO LONG BECAUSE OF IT. OH, HOW DIFFERENT AND GRAND LIFE FEELS NOW THAT I DON'T LIVE WITH THE SHAME OF BEING QUEER AND TRANSGENDER.

There's my cute partner!

Hi, Max, how's the conference so far?

BORING! I'm happy to be out of there and excited for our lunch date.

Okay, burger time?

Hell yeah, let's do it.

I'M GRATEFUL THAT I NO LONGER FIGHT AN INTERNAL BATTLE ABOUT WHO I AM, AND THAT I HAVE A LIFE PARTNER WHO SUPPORTS AND LOVES THE PERSON I AM.

THE CHURCH'S RELENTLESS PERSECUTION HAS LASTING EFFECTS ON ME AND OTHERS THAT I KNOW.

Thank you, baby.

MY RELIGION'S RELENTLESSLY RIGID BELIEF SYSTEM CAUSED ME A LOT OF TRAUMA, BUT I STILL CONNECT SOME OF MY FONDEST MEMORIES TO THE CHURCH—ESPECIALLY AROUND MUSIC.

I WENT TO A LOT OF CHRISTIAN CONCERTS AND CONVENTIONS WHEN I WAS YOUNGER, AND I WAS THE BASSIST FOR THE YOUTH GROUP BAND. I RECALL LOOKING UP "GAY GOSPEL MUSIC" ONCE. THAT'S HOW I FOUND OUT ABOUT WILMER "LITTLE AX" BROADNAX.

Two for lunch?

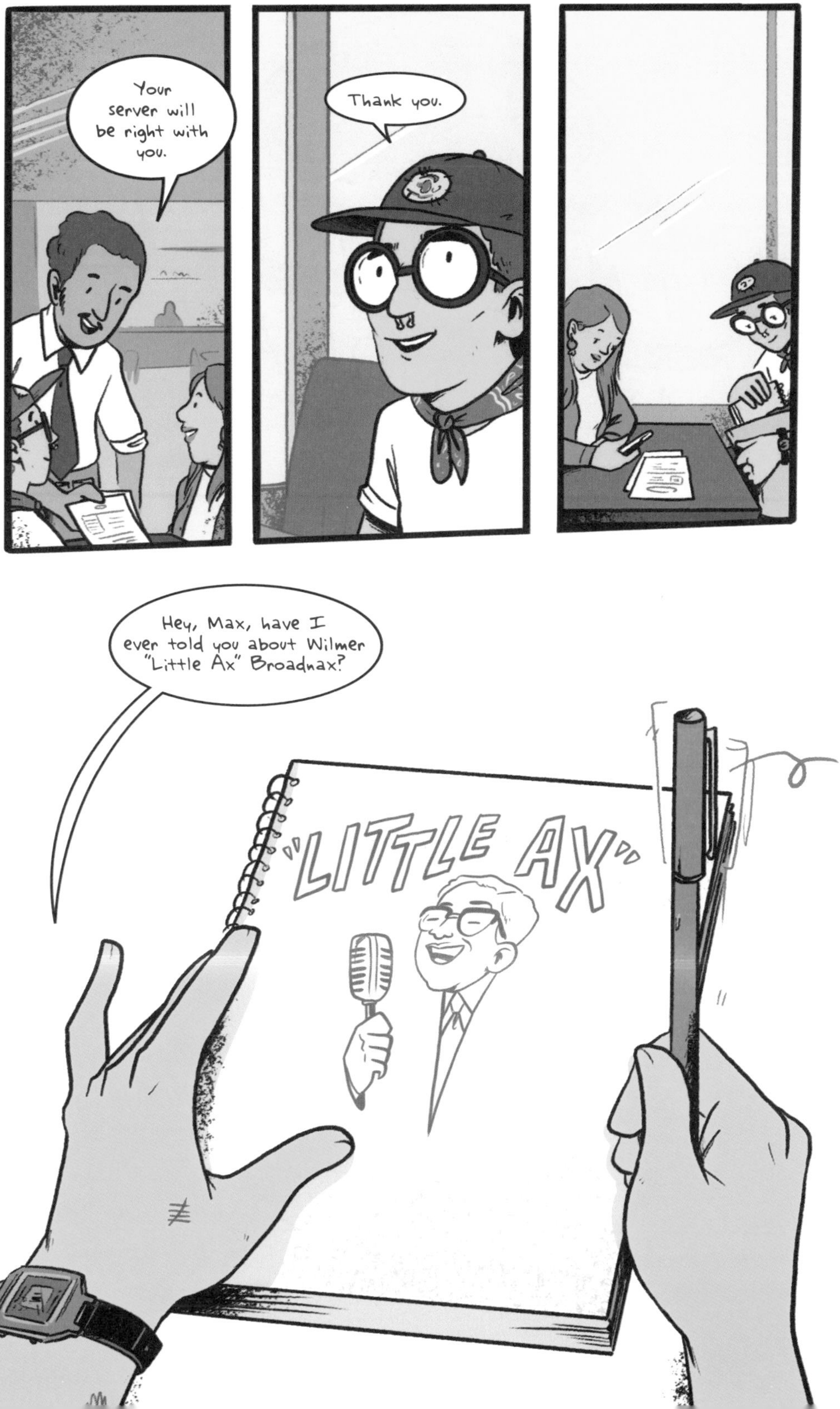
Your server will be right with you.
Thank you.
Hey, Max, have I ever told you about Wilmer "Little Ax" Broadnax?
"LITTLE AX"

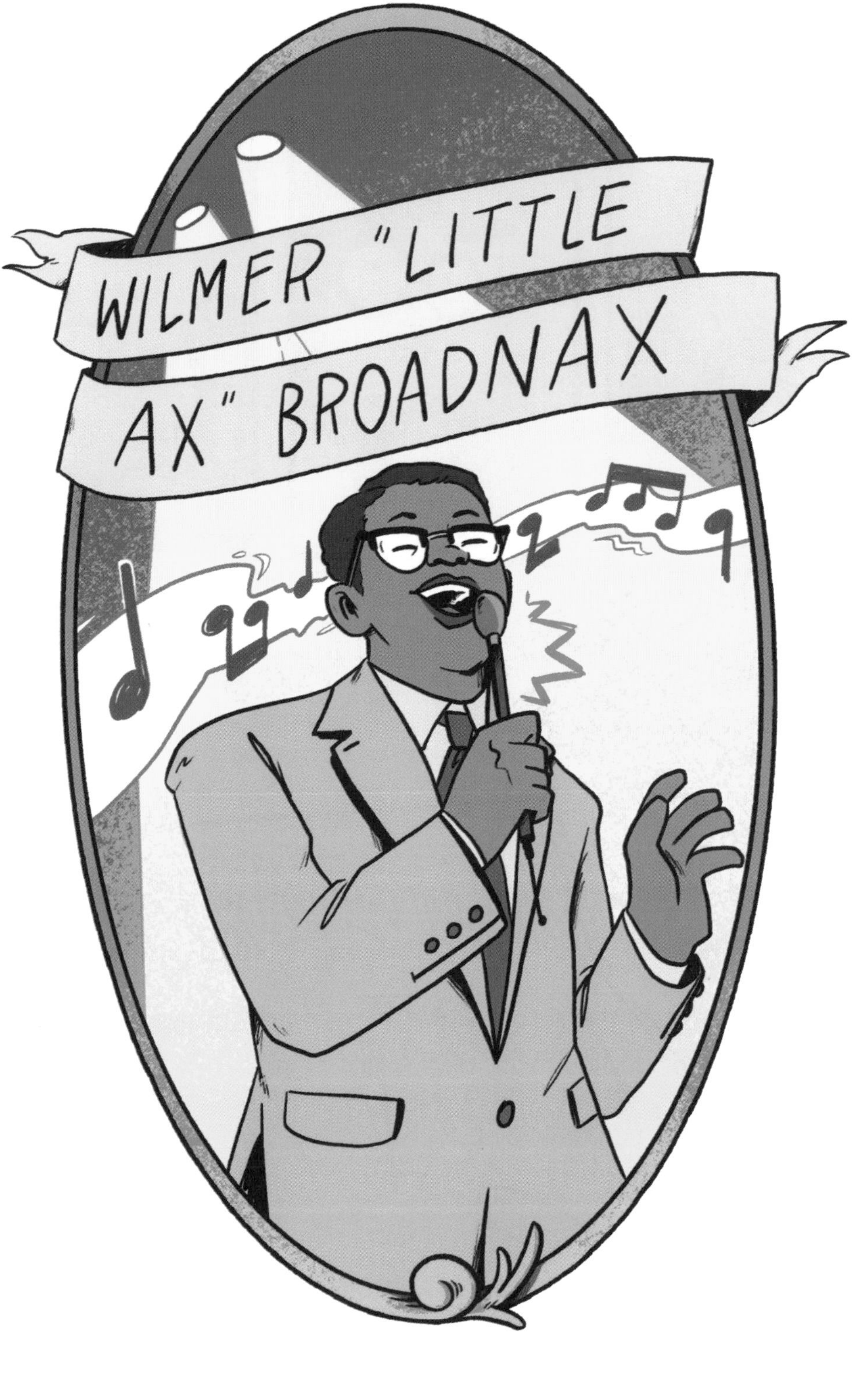
WILMER "LITTLE
AX" BROADNAX

WILMER "LITTLE AX" BROADNAX WAS BORN IN EITHER HOUSTON, TEXAS, OR SOMEWHERE IN LOUISIANA AND ASSIGNED FEMALE.

WILMER'S ORIGIN STORY HAS A FEW PUZZLE PIECES THAT DON'T FIT TOGETHER. NO ONE KNOWS HIS EXACT BIRTH DATE DUE TO VARIED U.S. CENSUS RECORDINGS.

IN THE 1930 CENSUS, WILMER'S FATHER, AUGUSTUS FLOWERS, RECORDED HIMSELF, HIS WIFE, TWO STEPSONS, AND A DAUGHTER NAMED ARMATHA.

AFTER THE 1930 CENSUS, ALL OFFICIAL GOVERNMENT RECORDS OF ARMATHA DISAPPEARED. NOT EVEN A SOCIAL SECURITY NUMBER WAS LEFT BEHIND.

SOME SPECULATE THAT WHEN HER OLDER BROTHER WILLIAM DIED YOUNG, THEIR PARENTS CHANGED ARMATHA'S NAME TO WILMER IN HIS MEMORY.

THEY USED THE NICKNAME "LITTLE AX" FOR WILMER, AND THEN RAISED HIM AS A BOY.

WHEN THEY WERE YOUNG, WILMER "LITTLE AX" AND OLDER BROTHER WILLIAM "BIG AX" SANG IN THE ST. PAUL GOSPEL SINGERS GROUP. THEY GOT THEIR NICKNAMES BECAUSE OF THEIR DIFFERENCES IN VOICE AND HEIGHT.

NOBODY KNOWS THE TROUBLE I'VE SEEN

NOBODY KNOWS BUT JESUS

WILLIAM WAS "BIG AX" BECAUSE HE WAS TALL AND BARITONE.

GLORY, GLORY HALLELUJAH!

WILMER WAS "LITTLE AX" BECAUSE HE WAS SHORT AND TENOR.

IN 1940, THEY MOVED TO LOS ANGELES TO SING WITH THE SOUTHERN GOSPEL SINGERS.

ALL OF THE SINGERS IN THE GROUP HAD DAY JOBS, SO TOURING WAS HARD.

BUT WILMER WANTED TO SING! SO HE LEFT THE GROUP AND FORMED THE GOLDEN ECHOES.

OF COURSE, HE LET HIS BROTHER, BIG AX, SING IN HIS GROUP.

SOON, THEY SIGNED WITH **SPECIALTY RECORDS**, THE SAME LABEL THAT PUT OUT RECORDS BY LITTLE RICHARD, JOHN LEE HOOKER, AND SAM COOKE.

WILMER, WITH HIS BROTHER, BOUNCED AROUND AMERICA, PERFORMING WITH SOME OF THE BIGGEST GOSPEL GROUPS OF THE 1950S AND '60S.

AS THE GOLDEN AGE OF GOSPEL WAS DYING DOWN, AND ROCK 'N' ROLL BEGAN TO TAKE OVER THE MUSIC CHARTS, WILMER RENAMED THE GROUP LITTLE AX & HIS GOLDEN ECHOES. HE HOPED A NEW NAME WOULD BRING IN NEW LISTENERS.

BUT WILMER NEVER MADE THE JUMP TO SECULAR MUSIC. A SHIFT IN THE MUSIC INDUSTRY TURNED MAINSTREAM ATTENTION TO THE BRITISH INVASION.

LITTLE AX QUIT.

HE LIVED IN PHILADELPHIA WITH HIS GIRLFRIEND, LAVINA RICHARDSON, WHO WAS THIRTY YEARS HIS JUNIOR, WHEN HIS STORY TOOK A TRAGIC TURN.

OUT DRIVING ONE DAY, WILMER CAUGHT LAVINA OUT WITH ANOTHER MAN. HE CHASED THEM DOWN AND BUMPED THEM WITH HIS CAR.

THE INCIDENT ESCALATED WHEN WILMER THREATENED LAVINA WITH A KNIFE.

Are you cheating on me!?

LAVINA GOT HOLD OF THE KNIFE AND STABBED WILMER THREE TIMES.

A WEEK LATER, AT THE AGE OF 72, WILMER DIED.

Wilmer. Give me that!

SWIPE!

NO ONE IN WILMER'S LIFE KNEW HE WAS ASSIGNED FEMALE AT BIRTH UNTIL HE DIED.

IT IS ALSO NOT KNOWN IF WILMER EVER IDENTIFIED AS TRANSGENDER OR QUEER.

WILMER AND HIS BROTHER KEPT HIS SEX A SECRET ALL OF HIS LIFE.

WHEN NEWS OF HIS SEX CAME OUT IN HIS OBITUARY, IT SENT WAVES OF SHOCK THROUGH THE GOSPEL COMMUNITY, ERASING HIS IDENTITY AS A MAN.

SOME PEOPLE AFTER DEATH ARE OFTEN MISGENDERED BY THEIR FAMILIES, OUTED, OR OTHERWISE DISRESPECTED. THEIR BODY IS DRESSED IN GENDERED CLOTHING THEY WOULDN'T HAVE CHOSEN FOR THEMSELVES IN LIFE.

SOME FAMILIES ALSO BURY THEIR TRANSGENDER LOVED ONES UNDER DEAD NAMES.

I'M AFRAID OF THIS FOR MYSELF, AND FOR MY TRANS, INTERSEX, AND NONBINARY FRIENDS.

Hello, ladies. What are we drinking today?

A LOT OF OUR FAMILIES MISGENDER US NOW, SO WHY WOULD THAT CHANGE AFTER WE DIE?

I will have a Pibb and **they** will do a Coke Zero.

IF YOU OR A LOVED ONE ARE TRANSGENDER OR NONBINARY, **THE ORDER OF GOOD HEALTH**'S WEBSITE HAS INFORMATION ON HOW TO ENSURE RESPECT OF ONE'S GENDER AFTER DEATH.

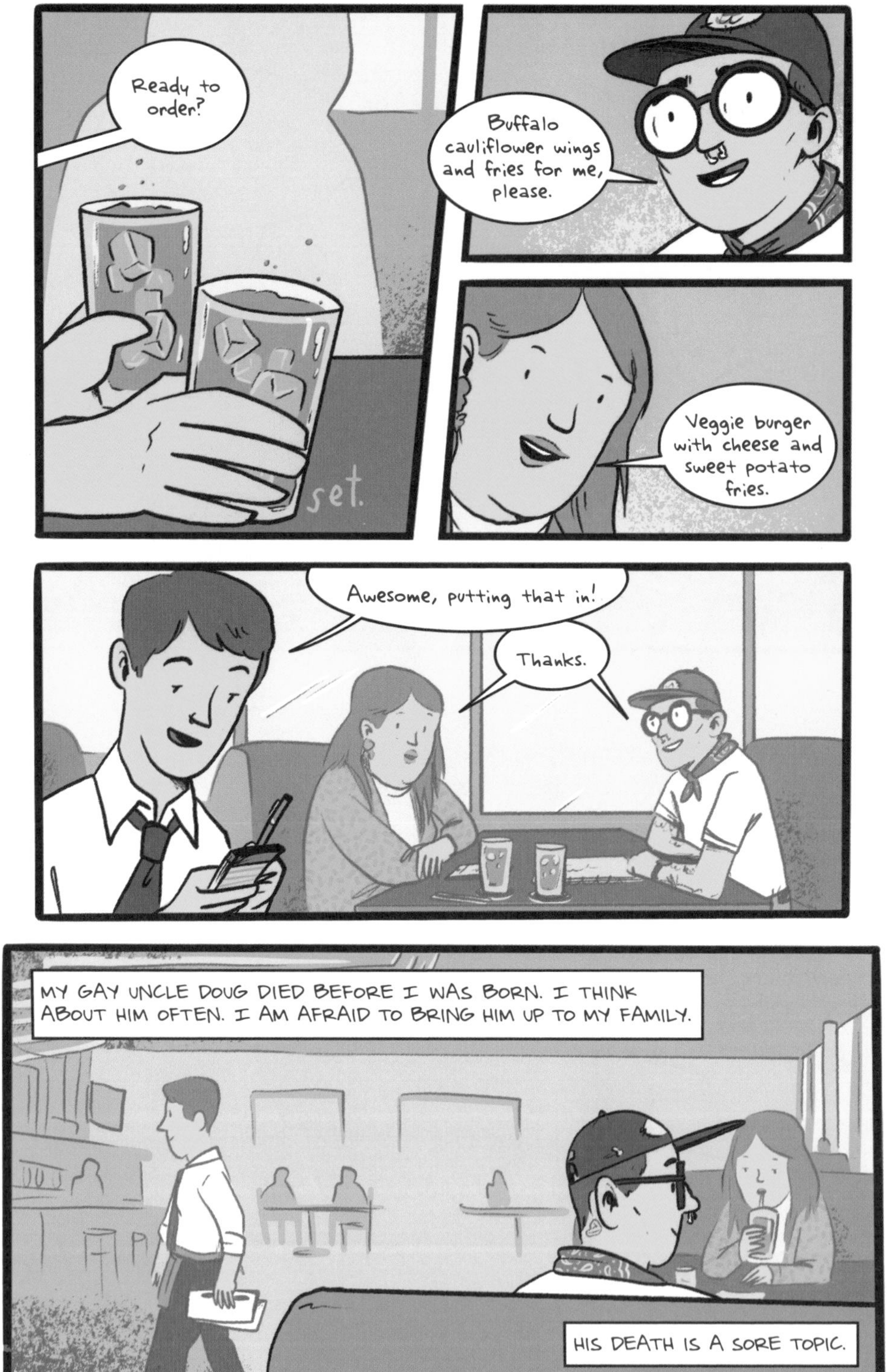
Ready to order?
set.
Buffalo cauliflower wings and fries for me, please.
Veggie burger with cheese and sweet potato fries.
Awesome, putting that in!
Thanks.
MY GAY UNCLE DOUG DIED BEFORE I WAS BORN. I THINK ABOUT HIM OFTEN. I AM AFRAID TO BRING HIM UP TO MY FAMILY.
HIS DEATH IS A SORE TOPIC.

IN 1981, A "RARE CANCER" WAS FIRST SEEN IN A GROUP OF GAY MEN AND EVENTUALLY BECAME AN EPIDEMIC.

AT THE TIME, LITTLE INFORMATION ON HOW ACQUIRED IMMUNE DEFICIENCY SYNDROME (AIDS) SPREAD, AND HOMOPHOBIA CAUSED A LOT OF PEOPLE TO DIE.

THIS VIRUS TOOK ITS TOLL ON MY OWN FAMILY, WHEN MY UNCLE DOUG, A GAY MAN, WAS DIAGNOSED WITH HIV IN THE LATE 1980s. A YEAR OR TWO LATER, HIS HIV TURNED INTO AIDS.

HE HELPED FOUND THE LOCAL SAN ANTONIO AIDS FOUNDATION WITH A FRIEND AND LIVED AND WORKED IN THE **"CASA DE CARE"** HOME THEY OWNED FOR THOSE DEALING WITH THE VIRUS, LIKE HIM.

HE DIED AT THE AGE OF 27 DUE TO COMPLICATIONS RELATED TO THE AIDS VIRUS.

DOUG'S LIFE AND ACTIVISM REMINDS ME OF SOMEONE ELSE.

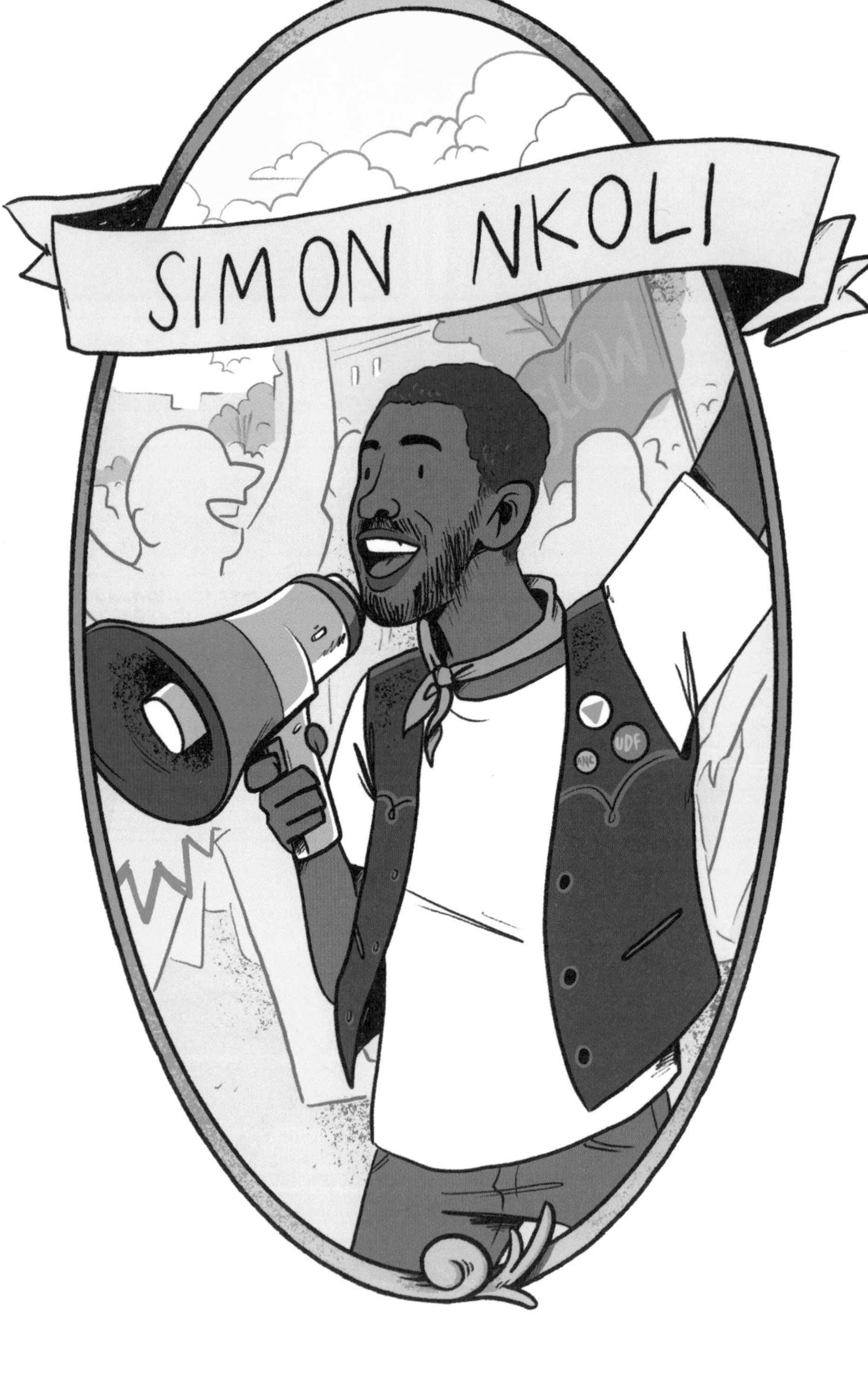
SIMON NKOLI
UDF

Let me preface Simon's story with a little bit of background!

He's from South Africa, under apartheid, which was a complex system of institutionalized racial segregation.

THOSE THAT UPHELD APARTHEID MADE SURE THAT THE POLITICAL, ECONOMIC, AND SOCIAL ASPECTS OF THEIR SOCIETY WERE NOT ONLY DOMINATED BY THE WHITE POPULATION, BUT BENEFITED THEM.

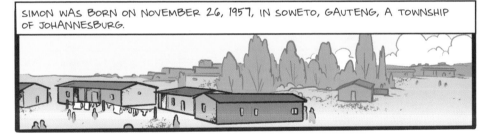

SIMON WAS BORN ON NOVEMBER 26, 1957, IN SOWETO, GAUTENG, A TOWNSHIP OF JOHANNESBURG.

MUCH OF HIS CHILDHOOD WAS SPENT HIDING FROM POLICE ENFORCING "PASS LAWS," WHICH RESTRICTED WHERE BLACK CITIZENS COULD LIVE.

ONE OF SIMON'S MOST VIVID CHILDHOOD MEMORIES INVOLVED HIDING HIS PARENTS IN A WARDROBE FROM THE POLICE AT AGE NINE.

HIS PARENTS SEPARATED WHEN HE WAS YOUNG, AND HE WAS SENT TO LIVE WITH HIS GRANDPARENTS, TENANT FARMERS ON A WHITE-OWNED ESTATE.

SIMON FOUND THE WORK MUNDANE. HE CRAVED KNOWLEDGE, SO HE ENROLLED IN SCHOOL WHILE CONTINUING TO WORK ON THE FARM.

WHEN HIS GRANDFATHER NEEDED EXTRA LABOR TO HELP PAY THE LANDLORD, HE TRIED CONVINCING SIMON TO QUIT SCHOOL.

WHEN HE WAS 19, SIMON WROTE TO ANDRE, A SOON-TO-BE-BOY-FRIEND HE MET THROUGH AN AD IN A PEN PAL MAGAZINE.

ANDRE WAS A WHITE BUS DRIVER WHO ALSO HAPPENED TO LIVE IN JOHANNESBURG. HIS FAMILY KNEW AND ACCEPTED THAT HE WAS GAY, BUT THEY WOULD NOT ALLOW HIM TO BE WITH A BLACK MAN.

SIMON, IN THE MEANTIME, COULDN'T KEEP HIS DESIRES A SECRET ANY LONGER AND TOLD HIS MOTHER HE WAS GAY. SHE WAS UPSET.

SIMON'S MOTHER FORCED HIM TO CONSULT PRIESTS, DOCTORS, AND PSYCHIATRISTS TO "CURE" HIS HOMOSEXUALITY.

Repeat after me,

"I am not gay. God made me in his image to be straight."

TODAY, A LOT OF FAMILIES ALL OVER THE WORLD PUT THEIR LGBTQ+ LOVED ONES THROUGH TRAUMATIC CONVERSION THERAPIES TO "CONVERT" THEM INTO BEING WHAT THEY DEEM AS NORMAL.

ANDRE AND SIMON WERE DEVASTATED BY THEIR FAMILIES' REACTION TO THEIR RELATIONSHIP.

BUT SIMON'S MOTHER, AFRAID OF NEVER SEEING HER SON AGAIN IF SHE DIDN'T TRY TO UNDERSTAND, EVENTUALLY ALLOWED HIM IN HER LIFE AGAIN IF HE PROMISED TO SEE A PSYCHIATRIST.

I am not sure I could ever live without you.

IT TURNED OUT THE PSYCHIATRIST WAS GAY, TOO. HE HELPED THE COUPLE FIGURE OUT HOW TO LIVE TOGETHER IN SECRET AT COLLEGE BY SUGGESTING SIMON POSE AS ANDRE'S PERSONAL SERVANT.

IN COLLEGE, SIMON WAS ARRESTED FOUR TIMES IN 1976 ALONE FOR PROTESTING APARTHEID.

HE JOINED THE CONGRESS OF SOUTH AFRICAN STUDENTS, WHICH AIMED TO END APARTHEID.

C.O.S.A.

WHEN THE GROUP CAUGHT WIND OF SIMON'S SEXUALITY, THEY DEBATED WHETHER OR NOT TO KICK HIM OUT.

THEY DIDN'T.

AFTER SIMON AND ANDRE BROKE UP, FEW RESOURCES FOR GAY MEN EXISTED. THOSE THAT DID CATERED TO WHITE PEOPLE, AND MOST OF THE GAY VENUES WERE IN DISTRICTS ZONED FOR WHITE PEOPLE.

EUROPEANS BLANKES

SIMON STILL JOINED THE GAY ASSOCIATION OF SOUTH AFRICA AS ITS FIRST BLACK MEMBER.

UNLIKE SIMON, THE GROUP TOOK AN APOLITICAL STANCE ON APARTHEID, PERHAPS BECAUSE ITS ALL-WHITE MEMBERSHIP FELT THE BENEFITS OF IT.

Why do you even bother with anti-apartheid stuff, Simon?

THEIR AGNOSTIC VIEW ON APARTHEID CREATED TENSION WHEN SIMON ATTEMPTED TO MOVE THE GROUP'S MEETINGS OUT OF A WHITE-ONLY BUILDING. THEY WOULDN'T BUDGE.

All I'm saying is if you move our group meetings to a more inclusive area, then Black gay men will be able to attend.

SIMON THEN DECIDED TO FORM A BLACK GAY ORGANIZATION, THE SATURDAY GROUP.

Good morning, guys!

HE ALSO JOINED THE AFRICAN NATIONAL CONGRESS AND UNITED DEMOCRATIC FRONT (U.D.F.), BOTH ANTI-APARTHEID POLITICAL GROUPS.

THE U.D.F. TACKLED THE FIGHT AGAINST RENT HIKES.

SIMON FOUGHT AGAINST GOVERNMENT-IMPOSED RENT HIKES IN BLACK COMMUNITIES.

AT ONE DEMONSTRATION, THE PROTESTERS WERE TAKEN INTO POLICE CUSTODY AND CHARGED WITH "SUBVERSION, CONSPIRACY, AND TREASON," ALL OF WHICH WERE PUNISHABLE BY DEATH.

SIMON WAS DETAINED IN PRISON FOR NINE MONTHS, AND EVENTUALLY RELEASED ON BAIL AS TRIALS FOR THE PROTEST CONTINUED.

I declare this case as invalid.

AFTER AN APPEAL BASED ON A TECHNICALITY, THE TRIALS WERE CONSIDERED INVALID AND SIMON WAS ACQUITTED OF ALL CHARGES AGAINST HIM.

AFTER HIS DETAINMENT, SIMON WAS BANNED FROM JOINING HIS PREVIOUS ACTIVIST GROUPS WHO THOUGHT HE WOULD ATTRACT ATTENTION FROM THE GOVERNMENT.

REALIZING HE WAS AN OUTSIDER IN THE QUEER COMMUNITY, TOO, SIMON FOUNDED THE...

GAY + LESBIAN ORGANISATION OF THE WITWATERSRAND

G.L.O.W. PUT TOGETHER THE COUNTRY'S FIRST THREE PRIDE MARCHES. THEIR WORK IN THE COMMUNITY WAS A BEACON IN THE NIGHT, AS SMALLER TOWNSHIPS CREATED SIMILAR ORGANIZATIONS.

GLOW

LESBIANS + GAYS AGAINST APARTHEID

SIMON MET WITH THE ANTI-APARTHEID PRESIDENT OF SOUTH AFRICA, NELSON MANDELA, TO DISCUSS THE TREATMENT OF BLACK QUEER PEOPLE. EVENTUALLY, SOUTH AFRICA BECAME THE FIRST NATION TO INCLUDE "SEXUAL ORIENTATION" IN ITS CONSTITUTION'S ANTI-DISCRIMINATION CLAUSE. THEY ALSO INVALIDATED SODOMY LAWS AND LEGALLY RECOGNIZED QUEER RELATIONSHIPS.

Keep in touch, Simon. It was nice meeting you.

Holy crap, Nelson Mandela knows my name.

SOON AFTER, SIMON FOUND OUT THAT HE WAS HIV POSITIVE.

Say cheese!

SIMON'S FIGHTING SPIRIT WAS STRONG. HE CREATED THE TOWNSHIP AIDS PROJECT AND THE GAY MEN'S HEALTH FORUM, BOTH OF WHICH BROUGHT ABOUT AIDS EDUCATION AND COUNSELING.

Okay now, let's get to work. I want every single gay man in South Africa to get at least ten of these condoms.

IN 1998, HE DIED IN JOHANNESBURG WHEN HIS HIV PROGRESSED TO FULL-BLOWN AIDS.

FRIENDS, FELLOW ACTIVISTS, AND FAMILY PACKED HIS FUNERAL TO SHOW THEIR LOVE FOR THE WORK HE DID AND WHAT HE GAVE TO HIS COMMUNITY.

IN 1999, THE PRIDE PARADE IN JOHANNESBURG WAS DEDICATED TO SIMON AND A STREET CORNER ESTABLISHED IN HIS NAME.

SIMON WORKED CONSTANTLY FOR THE FAIR AND JUST TREATMENT OF HIS COMMUNITY.

HIS STRUGGLE TURNED INTO TRIUMPH THROUGH ACTIVISM.

I WANT TO CONTINUE SPEAKING OF THE PEOPLE THAT CAME BEFORE US IN QUEER HISTORY AND IN MY FAMILY, LIKE MY UNCLE DOUG AND HIS LESBIAN SISTER, MY AUNT CHERYL, WHO USED TO TALK TO ME ABOUT MY FEELINGS.

Thankfully, my aunt Cheryl and Jeannie both have some of Doug's stuff.

All right folks, food is up! Y'all enjoy.

Thanks, it looks great.

So, what do you think you have gotten out of drawing queer and trans icons from history?

They've shown me that queer, radical love and gender expressions that differ from the norm are perfectly fine.

The Gay and Lesbian Memory in Action archive that I've been using for research stated, "Without queer history, there is no queer pride." If LGBTQ+ people before us didn't strive to live as their authentic selves, we might not be able to be seen sharing a meal right now, much less in a relationship.

I know I would be a much sadder person, stuck in the closet.

Me too, and I wouldn't know about my gender.

I'd be a girl!

I love the person that you are today.

And I love the person you are.

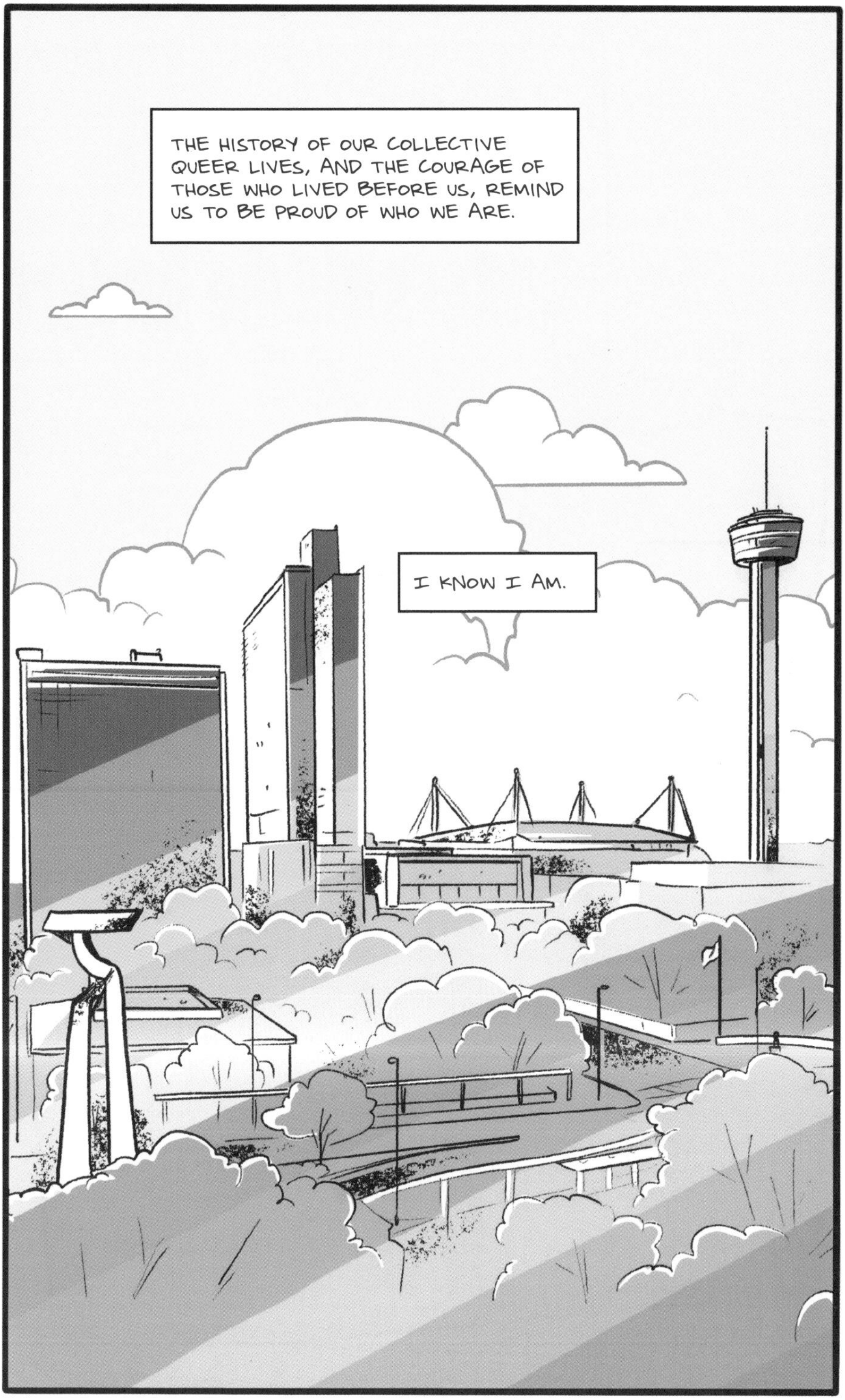
THE HISTORY OF OUR COLLECTIVE QUEER LIVES, AND THE COURAGE OF THOSE WHO LIVED BEFORE US, REMIND US TO BE PROUD OF WHO WE ARE.
I KNOW I AM.

Sozialhygienische Filmwerke

San.-Rat Dr. Magnus Hirschfeld

II.

Anders als die Andern

(§ 175)

PERSONEN:

Paul Faber, Violinvirtuose . . Conradt Veidt
Sein Vater . . . . Leo Connard
Seine Mutter . . . . Ilse v. Tasso-Lind
Sein Bruder . . . . Ernsi Pittschau
Dessen Frau . . . . Alexandra Wiellegh
Kurt Sivers . . . . Fritz Schulz
Else, seine Schwester . . . . Anita Berber
Sein Vater . . . . Wilhelm Diegelmann
Seine Mutter . . . . Clementine Plessner
Philipp Cisowsky . . . . . . Reinhold Schünzel
...n Gelehrier . . . . * * *

Regie: Richard Oswald

Richard Oswald-Film

My Sources...

GAYS FOR SOCIALISM

NANCY CÁRDENAS

Buffington, Rob. "Los Jotos: Contested Visions of Homosexuality in Modern Mexico." In Sex and Sexuality in Latin America, ed. Daniel Balderston and Donna J. Guy. 118–132. New York: New York University Press, 1997.

Carr, Barry, et al. Los Intelectuales y El Poder En Mexico: Memorias De La VI Conferencia De Historiadores Mexicanos y Estadounidenses = Intellectuals and Power in Mexico, edited by Roderic A Camp, Collegio De Mexico, University of California, Los Angeles, 1991, pp. 377–394.

Darling, Laura. "Nancy Cárdenas Part I." Making Queer History, Making Queer History, www.makingqueerhistory.com/ artcles/2020/4/29/nancy-crdenas-part-i.

"First Out Lesbian in Mexico." Champions: Biographies of Global LGBTQ Pioneers: Notebook, by M. Bonham, Bonham, 2014, p.42.

Garcia, Angelica, and Alberto Figueroa. "Nancy Cárdenas. Genero y Escena." Inba Digital, CONACULTA / INBA-CITRU, 1 Jan. 1970, inbadigital.bellasartes.gob.mx: 8080/jspui/ handle/11271/475.

Grinnell, Lucinda. "'Lesbianas Presente:' Lesbian Activism, Transnational Alliances, and the State in Mexico City, 1968–1991." UNM Digital Repository, University of New Mexico, 2014, digitalrepository.unm.edu/cgi/viewcontent.cgi? article=1034&context=hist_etds.

Ibanez, Alma. "Nancy Cárdenas y El Camino Hacia La Libertad." It Gets Better Mexico, itgetsbetter.org/mexico/initiatives/nancy/.

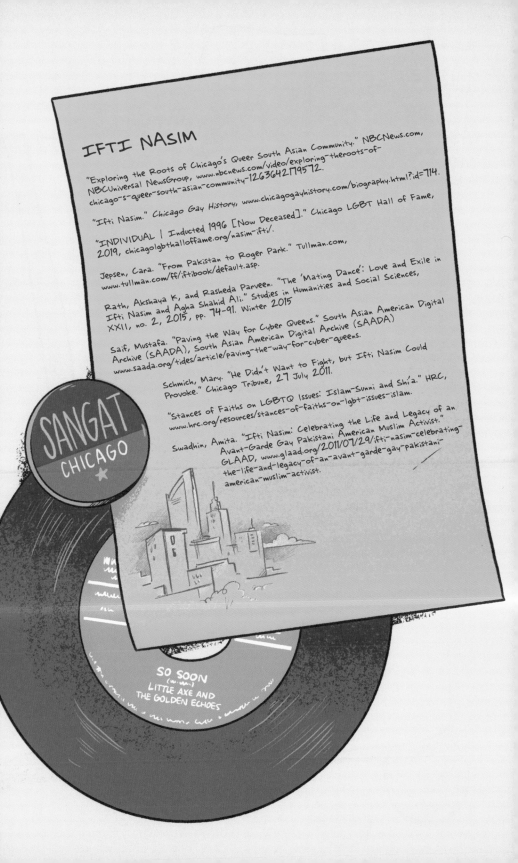

IFTI NASIM

"Exploring the Roots of Chicago's Queer South Asian Community." NBCNews.com, NBCUniversal NewsGroup, www.nbcnews.com/video/exploring-the-roots-of-chicago-s-queer-south-asian-community-1263642779572.

"Ifti Nasim." Chicago Gay History, www.chicagogayhistory.com/biography.html?id=714.

"INDIVIDUAL | Inducted 1996 [Now Deceased]." Chicago LGBT Hall of Fame, 2019, chicagolgbthalloffame.org/nasim-ifti/.

Jepsen, Cara. "From Pakistan to Roger Park." Tullman.com, www.tullman.com/ff/iftibook/default.asp.

Rath, Akshaya K, and Rasheda Parveen. "The 'Mating Dance': Love and Exile in Ifti Nasim and Agha Shahid Ali." Studies in Humanities and Social Sciences, XXII, no. 2, 2015, pp. 74-91. Winter 2015

Saif, Mustafa. "Paving the Way for Cyber Queens." South Asian American Digital Archive (SAADA), South Asian American Digital Archive (SAADA) www.saada.org/tides/article/paving-the-way-for-cyber-queens.

Schmich, Mary. "He Didn't Want to Fight, but Ifti Nasim Could Provoke." Chicago Tribune, 27 July 2011.

"Stances of Faiths on LGBTQ Issues: Islam-Sunni and Shi'a." HRC, www.hrc.org/resources/stances-of-faiths-on-lgbt-issues-islam.

Swadhin, Amita. "Ifti Nasim: Celebrating the Life and Legacy of an Avant-Garde Gay Pakistani American Muslim Activist." GLAAD, www.glaad.org/2011/07/29/ifti-nasim-celebrating-the-life-and-legacy-of-an-avant-garde-gay-pakistani-american-muslim-activist.

SO SOON
(ni-ini)
LITTLE AXE AND
THE GOLDEN ECHOES

SISTER ROSETTA THARPE

Diaz-Hurtado, Jessica. "Forebears: Sister Rosetta Tharpe, The Godmother of Rock 'N' Roll." NPR, NPR, 24 Aug. 2017, www.npr.org/2017/08/24/544226085/forebears-sister-rosetta-tharpe-the-godmother-of-rock-n-roll.

Lorusso, Marissa. "How One Of Music's Biggest Stars Almost Disappeared, And How Her Legacy Was Saved." NPR, NPR, 27 Sept. 2019, www.npr.org/2019/09/27/759601364/how-one-of-musics-biggest-stars-almost-disappeared-and-how-her-legacy-was-saved.

NPR, Ari Shapiro. "'The Most Elaborate Wedding Ever Staged': Rosetta Tharpe at Griffith Stadium." KPBS Public Media, KPBS, 25 Sept. 2019, www.kpbs.org/news/2019/sep/25/the-most-elaborate-wedding-ever-staged-rosetta/.

Rose, Caryn. "She Can Make That Guitar Talk." NPR, NPR, 24 Sept. 2019, www.npr.org/2019/09/24/759600717/she-can-make-that-guitar-talk.

"Sister Rosetta Tharpe." Rock & Roll Hall of Fame, 2018, www.rockhall.com/inductees/sister-rosetta-tharpe.

Wald, Gayle. Shout, Sister, Shout!: The Untold Story of Rock-and-Roll Trailblazer Sister Rosetta Tharpe. Beacon, 2008.

White, Erin. "QUEER, BLACK & BLUE: SISTER ROSETTA THARPE IS MUVA OF THEM ALL." AFROPUNK, 7 Mar. 2019, afropunk.com/2019/03/rosetta-tharpe/.

WE'WHA

BAE GN SI 3641, National Anthropological Archives, Smithsonian Institution.

Kallestewa Jr, Gilbert. Information Engineering Technology. "KESHI! WELCOME." Pueblo of Zuni, www.ashiwi.org/.

Nichols, Lynn. "Zuni Accusative Intransitives." *International Journal of American Linguistics*, vol. 74, no. 1, 2008, pp. 115–116., doi:10.1086/529465.

Outlines of Zuni Creation Myths, by Frank Hamilton. Cushing, U.S. G.P.O., 1896, pp. 398–402.

Kaldera, Raven. "Ergi: The Way of the Third." Northern-Tradition Shamanism. https://web.archive.orgweb/201305 0115 2328/http://www.northernshamanism.org/ shamanic-techniques/gender-sexuality/ergi-the-way-of-the-third.html

Roscoe, Will. *The Zuni Man-Woman*. University of New Mexico Press, 1991.

Smith, Amelia. "WE'WHA: AN EXPLORATION INTO AGENCY." MUSINGS, musingsmmst.blogspot.com/2020/04/wewha-exploration-into-agency.html.

Smithsonian Institution Archives, Acc. 11-006, Box 009, Image No. MAH-3648.

Swan-Perkins, Samuel White. "5 Two-Spirit Heroes Who Paved the Way for Today's Native LGBTQ+ Community." KQED, 20 Nov. 2018, www.kqed.org/arts/13845330/ 5-two-spirit-heroes-who-paved-the-way-for-todays-native-lgbtq-community.

"Weiwha-Gender and Sexuality Student Services." University of Illinois Springfield, www.uis.edu/gender sexualitystudentservices/weiwha/.

Willams, Walter L. "The Berdache Tradition." University of California San Diego. UCSD Lecture Notes, 2000.

Zuni Indians: Their Mythology, Esoteric Fraternities, and Ceremonies, by Matilda Coxe. Stevenson, Nabu Press, 2010.

MARY
JONES

"Announcing the Release of Salacia, a New Film by Tourmaline." Barnard Center for Research on Women, 26 Apr. 2019, bcrw.barnard.edu/announcing-the-release-of-salacia-a-new-film-by-tourmaline/.

Center for Lesbian and Gay Studies, City University of New York, and Jonathan Ned Katz. Queer Representations: Reading Lives, Reading Cultures (A Center for Lesbian and Gay Studies Book) / Edition 1: Paperback.

"Digital Transgender Archive." Illustration of Mary Jones (1838) – Digital Transgender Archive, 1836, www.digitaltransgenderarchive.net/files/q237hs14t.

"Gender Bending in 19th Century New York." MCNY Blog: New York Stories, 12 July 2011, blog.mcny.org/2011/07/12/gender-bending-in-19th-century-new-york/.

Katz, Jonathan Ned, and Tavia Nyong'o. "The 'Man-Monster' by Jonathan Ned Katz • Peter Sewally/Mary Jones,June 11, 1836 • OutHistory: It's About Time." Outhistory.org, outhistory.org/exhibits/show/sewally-jones/man-monster.

"Mary Jones AKA Beefsteak Pete." The Oldest Profession Podcast, theoldestprofessionpodcast.com/mary-jones-aka-beefsteak-pete/.

McNally, Deborah. "Five Points District, New York City, New York (1830s-1860s)." Welcome to Blackpast •, 2 Dec. 2007, www.blackpast.org/african-american-history/five-points-district-new-york-city-1830s-1860s/.

Nyong'o, Tavia. The Amalgamation Waltz: Race, Performance, and the Ruses of Memory. Univ. of Minnesota Press, 2009.

MAGNUS HIRSCHFELD

Berlin, Magnus-Hirschfeld-Gesellschaft e.V., and Harald Rimmele. Institute for Sexual Science (1919-1933) - Online-Exhibition by the Magnus-Hirschfeld Society, Berlin, www.hirschfeld.in-berlin.de/institut/en/ifsframe.html?personen%2Fpers_33.html.

Dose, Ralf. Magnus Hirschfeld: Deutscher, Jude, Weltburger. Hentrich & Hentrich, 2005.

Dose, Ralf. "Thirty Years of Collecting Our History— Or: How to Find Treasure Troves." ALMS Conference, Amsterdam, 1 Aug. 2012.

Dutton, Ron. "The Mystery of Li Shiu Tong." Xtra, 15 Oct. 2003, www.dailyxtra.com/the-mystery-of-li-shiu-tong-43055.

Green, David B. "1868: The 'Einstein of Sex' Is Born (and Dies)." Haaretz.com, Haaretz.com, 13 May 2015, www.haaretz.com/jewish/.premium-1868-the-einstein-of-sex-is-born-and-dies-1.5361786.

Hirschfeld, Magnus, and James J. Conway. Berlin's Third Sex. Rixdorf, 2017.

Nazi Persecution of Homosexuals Exhibition, United States Holocaust Memorial Museum.

"Magnus-Hirschfeld-Gesellschaft." Magnus Hirschfeld Und Das Institut Fur Sexualwissenschaft, magnus-hirschfeld.de/start-en/.

McLeod, Donald W. "Serendipity and the Papers of Magnus Hirschfeld: The Case of Ernst Maass." doi:https://tspace.library.utoronto.ca/bitstream/1807/32968/1/Maass.pdf.

Melville, Raymond. "Dr. Magnus Hirschfeld." Famous GLBT & GLBTI People, Stonewall Society, www.stonewallsociety.com/famouspeople/magnus.htm.

Peter Tatchell Foundation. "Magnus Hirschfeld 1868-1935: German LGBT Pioneer." Peter Tatchell Foundation, 22 Feb. 2018, www.petertatchellfoundation.org/magnus-hirschfeld-1868-1935-german-lgbt-pioneer/.

CARLETT BROWN

Blackout. *Black on Both Sides: A Racial History of Trans Identity*, by C. Riley Snorton, University of Minnesota Press, 2017.

"Carlett Brown: The Extreme Marginalization of Transwomen of Color • Challenging Gender Boundaries: A Trans Biography Project by Students of Dr. Catherine Jacquet • OutHistory: It's About Time." Outhistory.org, outhistory.org/exhibits/show/tgi-bios/carlett-brown.

"Digital Transgender Archive." Male Shake Dancer Plans to Change Sex, Wed GI in Europe – Digital Transgender Archive, *Jet Magazine*, 18 June 1953, www.digitaltransgenderarchive.net/files/zo29p484q.

"Digital Transgender Archive." Shake Dancer Postpones Sex Change for Face Lifting – Digital Transgender Archive, *Jet Magazine*, 6 Aug. 1953, www.digitaltransgenderarchive.net/files/b8515n46z.

"Digital Transgender Archive." Tax Snag Halts Male Dancer's Trip for Sex Change – Digital Transgender Archive, *Jet Magazine*, 15 Oct. 1953, www.digitaltransgenderarchive.net/files/xk8ljk50j.

"From GI Joe to GI Jane: Christine Jorgensen's Story: The National WWII Museum: New Orleans." The National WWII Museum | New Orleans, The National World War II Museum, 30 June 2020, www.nationalww2museum.org/war/articles/christine-jorgensen.

"Male Dancer Charles Brown Becomes Danish Citizen to Change His Sex." *Jet Magazine*, 25 June 1953.

Spark. "Category: Carlett A Brown." SPARK Reproductive Justice NOW, 27 Feb. 2017, www.sparkrj.org/category/carlett-a-brown/.

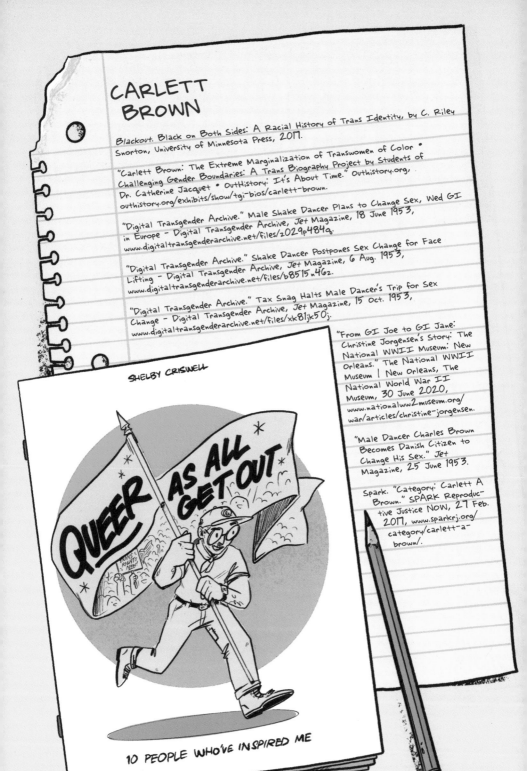

SHELBY CRISWELL

QUEER AS ALL GET OUT

10 PEOPLE WHO'VE INSPIRED ME

Pauli Murray

The Autobiography

of a Black Activist,

Feminist, Lawyer,

Priest, and Poet

DR. PAULI MURRAY

Downs, Kenya. "The 'Black, Queer, Feminist' Legal Trailblazer You've Never Heard Of." NPR, NPR, 19 Feb. 2015, www.npr.org/sections/codeswitch/2015/02/19/387200033/the-black-queer-feminist-legal-trailblazer-youve-never-heard-of.

Editorial Board. "Pauli Murray and the Pronominal Problem: a De-Essentialist Trans Historiography." The Activist History Review, 30 May 2019, activisthistory.com/2019/05/30/pauli-murray-and-the-pronominal-problem-a-de-essentialist-trans-historiography/.

"Finding Pauli Murray." National Organization for Women, now.org/about/history/finding-pauli-murray/.

"Imp, Crusader, Dude, Priest." Imp Crusader Dude Priest, sites.fhi.duke.edu/paulimurrayproject/timeline/.

Murray, Pauli, and Elizabeth Alexander. Dark Testament: and Other Poems. Liveright Publishing Corporation, a Division of W. W. Norton & Company, 2018.

Murray, Pauli, and Patricia Bell-Scott. Song in a Weary Throat: Memoir of an American Pilgrimage. Liveright Publishing Corporation, a Division of W.W. Norton Et Company, 2018.

Murray, Pauli. Pauli Murray: The Autobiography of a Black Activist, Feminist, Lawyer, Priest, and Poet. University of Tennessee Press, 2003.

Murray, Pauli. PROUD SHOES: The Story of an American Family. Beacon.

"Pronouns & Pauli Murray." Pauli Murray Center, www.paulimurraycenter.com/pronouns-pauli-murray.

Rosenberg, Rosalind. Jane Crow: The Life of Pauli Murray. Oxford University Press US, 2020.

Schulz, Kathryn. "The Civil-Rights Luminary You've Never Heard Of." The New Yorker, 10 Apr. 2017, www.newyorker.com/magazine/2017/04/17/the-many-lives-of-pauli-murray.

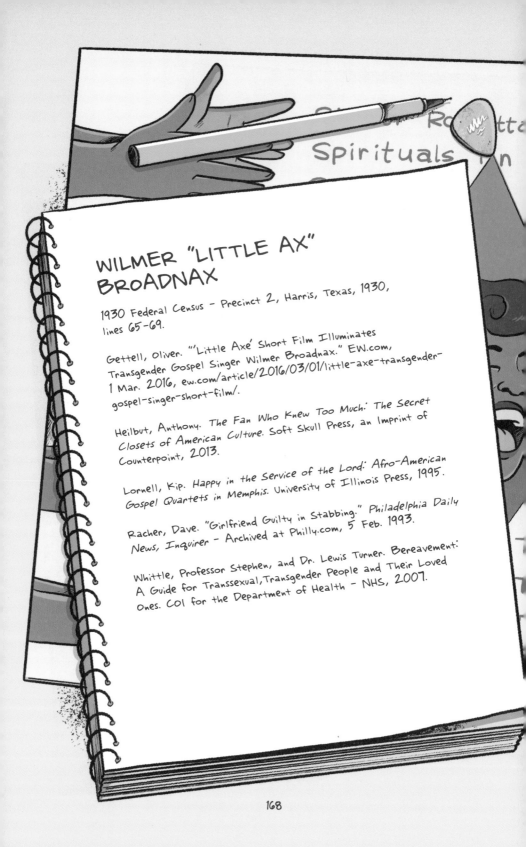

WILMER "LITTLE AX" BROADNAX

1930 Federal Census - Precinct 2, Harris, Texas, 1930, lines 65-69.

Gettell, Oliver. "'Little Axe' Short Film Illuminates Transgender Gospel Singer Wilmer Broadnax." EW.com, 1 Mar. 2016, ew.com/article/2016/03/01/little-axe-transgender-gospel-singer-short-film/.

Heilbut, Anthony. The Fan Who Knew Too Much: The Secret Closets of American Culture. Soft Skull Press, an Imprint of Counterpoint, 2013.

Lornell, Kip. Happy in the Service of the Lord: Afro-American Gospel Quartets in Memphis. University of Illinois Press, 1995.

Racher, Dave. "Girlfriend Guilty in Stabbing." Philadelphia Daily News, Inquirer - Archived at Philly.com, 5 Feb. 1993.

Whittle, Professor Stephen, and Dr. Lewis Turner. Bereavement: A Guide for Transsexual, Transgender People and Their Loved Ones. COI for the Department of Health - NHS, 2007.

SIMON NKOLI

Bella, Kyle. "Simon Nkoli's LGBT Activist Legacy." Our Viral Lives, ourviral lives.org/2016/01/08/simon-nkolis-lgbt-activist-legacy/.

Bella, Kyle. "Viral Fragment: Simon Nkoli." Our Viral Lives, ourvirallives.org/2016/08/16/viral-fragment-simon-nkoli/.

"Delmas Treason Trial 1985-1989." Historical Papers, Wits University, http://www.historicalpapers.wits.ac.za/?inventory/U/collections&c=AK2117/R/8206.

GALA. "Till the Time of Trial - The Prison Letters of Simon Knoli." Gay and Lesbian Memory in Action, gala.co.za/wp-content/uploads/2019/12/Till-the-time-of-trial-2007-nkoli.pdf.

McKellen, Ian. "Ian McKellen: Writings: Tribute: Nelson Mandela (1918-2013)." Ian McKellen | Writings | Tribute | Nelson Mandela (1918-2013), McKellen. com, 5 Dec. 2013, mckellen.com/writings/tribute/madiba.htm.

Nkoli, Simon. "This Strange Feeling." The Invisible Ghetto: Lesbian and Gay Writing from South Africa. Matthew Krouse and Kim Berman, eds. London: Gay Men's Press, 1995. 19-26.

"Simon and I." IMDb, IMDb.com, 4 Aug. 2002, www.imdb.com/title/tt0395763/.

"Simon Nkoli." Simon Nkoli | South African History Online, www.sahistory.org.za/people/simon-nkoli.

Scan this code on your Spotify app for the official *Queer As All Get Out* playlist!

RADICAL FAIRY

FIGHT AIDS, NOT PEOPLE WITH AIDS

LEEDS TOWN HALL 1957

GLOSSARY

Note that these terms and definitions are ever-changing and morphing with each new era. By the time of publication, some of these terms and their definitions might be outdated.

<u>To research up-to-date definitions:</u>

GLAAD Lesbian / Gay / Bisexual Glossary of Terms, www.glaad.org/reference/lgbtq

InterACT definition of Intersex, interactadvocates.org

Intersex Society of North America responds to commonly asked questions about Intersex people, isna.org/faq/

LGBTQIA Resource Center Glossary, lgbtqia.ucdavis.edu/educated/glossary

Montclair State University's LGBTQ Center Terminology Resource, www.montclair.edu/lgbtq-center/lgbtq-resources/terminology/

- **2SLGBTQIAP+ (or LGBT, LGBTQ, LGBTQ+)**
  An ever-changing and expanding acronym for non-heterosexual sexualities and gender-identities. The common acronym for this is LGBT or LGBTQ+. The plus on the end signifies that there are more sexualities and genders than the ones represented by the acronym: Two-Spirit, Lesbian, Gay, Bisexual or Bigender, Transgender, Queer, Intersex, Asexual, Pansexual, and so on.

  - **ASSIGNED GENDER OR ASSIGNED AT BIRTH GENDER**
    The gender appointed to a person at birth by their doctor, parents or legal guardian, typically based off of the genitalia with which they were born. Most often, the assigned gender is one of the two primary genders used in the Western binary societies: male or female.

- BISEXUAL

  A bisexual person is thought of as someone who is attracted to both men and women, but it can also mean someone who is attracted to someone of their same gender as well as other genders. Someone can be both bisexual and pansexual interchangeably (see definition for pansexual).

- CHOSEN FAMILY

  A term typically used within queer spaces to define a group of friends, lovers, or comrades that are seen as one's family over the biological one they were born into and share blood with. Rejection from one's biological/adopted family can lead to creating a chosen family.

- CISGENDER

  A term for a person whose gender identity matches the gender they were assigned at birth. A cisgender or cis person is not transgender.

- CROSS-DRESSING OR CROSS-DRESSER

  When an individual dresses in clothing that is not often associated with their assigned gender. Mostly this term is used for those that don't necessarily wish to transition genders, like a transgender person might. Cross-dressing is a means of gender expression rather than a sexuality.

- DEAD NAME OR DEAD-NAMING

  The name that someone was assigned at birth or their former name. Use of a dead name without someone's consent is called dead-naming. Intentional dead-naming is often considered deeply disrespectful and transphobic. It is sometimes used as an aggressive dismissal and rejection of another's gender identity.

- DYSPHORIA

  An internal conflict between one's physical body or assigned gender and the gender that they identify with. This affects people in many different ways, i.e., dressing, receiving gender-affirming surgeries or hormone therapy, altering one's look and or voice, assigning a new name, etc. This is not synonymous with gender nonconformity however, which refers to behaviors that don't match societal gender expectations, norms, and stereotypes of their assigned gender.

- DYKE, FAGGOT OR FAG

  Derogatory and outdated terms used against someone perceived as non-heteronormative. These terms are often used by queer people in a positive way to reclaim them from their slanderous roots.

Gender Expressions
Subscription form

		ADD	TOTAL
☐ 1 YEAR $30	☐ 1 YEAR FIRST CLASS	$12.50	$42.50
☐ 2 YEARS $54	☐ 2 YEARS FIRST CLASS	$25	$79

☐ Money Order   ☐ Check
Make check/money order payable to BISLEY ENTERPRISES

NAME _____

ADDRESS _____
_____

CITY _____ STATE _____ ZIP _____

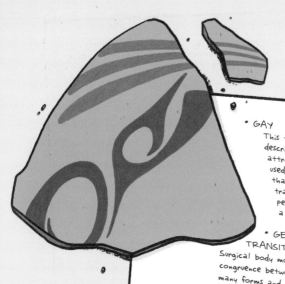

- GAY

This term has many meanings. At times it is used to describe queer people in general, or those that are attracted to the same sex. Other times it is exclusively used in reference to men (cisgender or transgender) that are attracted to other men (cisgender or transgender). Lesbians, bisexuals, and transgender people might feel excluded by the term, but this is a personal preference.

- GENDER-AFFIRMATION SURGERY OR TRANSITIONAL SURGERY

Surgical body modification that one might undergo to seek congruence between one's body and gender identity. This comes in many forms and is up to personal preference, i.e., vocal therapy, facial reconstruction, hormone therapy, breast implants, etc.

- GENDER BINARY

A division of gender that has been separated into two distinct and considered to be opposite categories: male and female. It is also seen as a social construct since there are more than just the "big two" gender identities that the binary claims.

- GENDERQUEER OR GENDER QUEER

An umbrella term that refers to non-heteronormative gender identities and expressions. This term is sometimes used by those that identify as holding queer or non-heteronormative qualities without placing a specific name on their gender. It has a similar scope and overlaps with the term nonbinary (see nonbinary).

- GENDER-VARIANT OR GENDER VARIANT

An umbrella term for gender identities and expressions that are different from societal, heteronormative norms. They fall within the transgender umbrella, like genderqueer and nonbinary identities, and don't fit within a two-gender binary.

- HERMAPHRODITE

An outdated term that implies someone is both fully male and fully female. This term is misleading. It is still used scientifically in reference to animals, but it is now a slur used against intersex people (see Intersex). Some intersex individuals use the term to reclaim it in a positive way. To read more about this term and why it is no longer necessary, please refer to the FAQ on the Intersex Society of North America's website (https://isna.org/faq/hermaphrodite/) as well as the FAQ on InterACT's website (https://interactadvocates.org/faq/).

Closets are Health Hazards

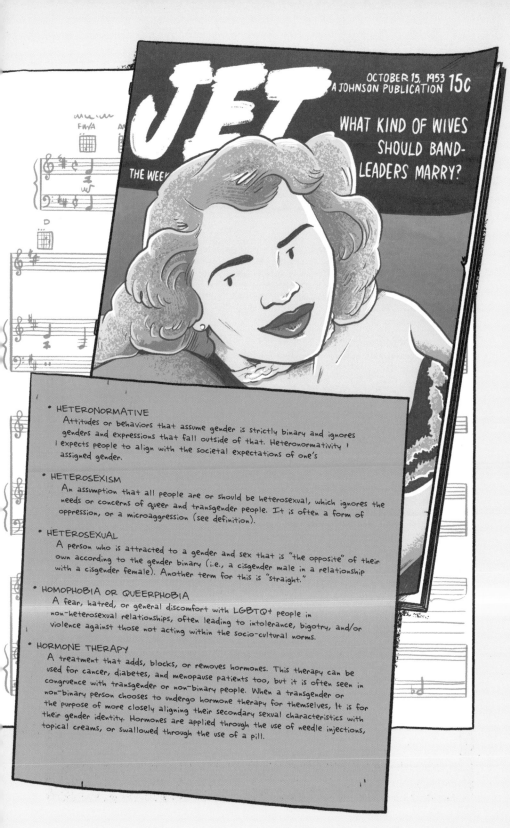

- HETERONORMATIVE

  Attitudes or behaviors that assume gender is strictly binary and ignores genders and expressions that fall outside of that. Heteronormativity expects people to align with the societal expectations of one's assigned gender.

- HETEROSEXISM

  An assumption that all people are or should be heterosexual, which ignores the needs or concerns of queer and transgender people. It is often a form of oppression, or a microaggression (see definition).

- HETEROSEXUAL

  A person who is attracted to a gender and sex that is "the opposite" of their own according to the gender binary (i.e., a cisgender male in a relationship with a cisgender female). Another term for this is "straight."

- HOMOPHOBIA OR QUEERPHOBIA

  A fear, hatred, or general discomfort with LGBTQ+ people in non-heterosexual relationships, often leading to intolerance, bigotry, and/or violence against those not acting within the socio-cultural norms.

- HORMONE THERAPY

  A treatment that adds, blocks, or removes hormones. This therapy can be used for cancer, diabetes, and menopause patients too, but it is often seen in congruence with transgender or non-binary people. When a transgender or non-binary person chooses to undergo hormone therapy for themselves, it is for the purpose of more closely aligning their secondary sexual characteristics with their gender identity. Hormones are applied through the use of needle injections, topical creams, or swallowed through the use of a pill.

- INTERSEX
  An umbrella term for differences in sex traits or reproductive anatomy and/or a
  chromosome pattern that doesn't fit the typical narrative of male or female.
  These traits are either present at birth or are developed later on into childhood.
  Often, intersex people undergo surgery at a young age that was chosen for them
  without their consent. This choice is often made out of shame and/or ignorance.
  Intersex people are not always part of the LGBTQ+ community, but may identify
  as such.

- MICROAGGRESSION
  A statement, action, or incident regarded as indirect or
  subtle discrimination against a marginalized group. An
  example of this is a straight person telling a gay man
  that he "doesn't sound like a gay man."

- NONBINARY OR GENDER NONBINARY
  Any gender identity that is not strictly male or female all
  of the time, either falling outside of the gender binary
  completely, or somewhere within the middle based on one's
  personal gender experience and identity.

- PANSEXUAL OR OMNISEXUAL
  A sexual identity for people that are attracted to all
  genders and sexes. There is a bit of an overlap between
  these terms and bisexuality (see bisexual).

- POLYAMORY OR POLYAMOROUS
  Being continually open to or in multiple romantic relationships
  at the same time, where all parties involved consent. This is a
  relationship status rather than a sexuality. An alternative to this
  is a monogamous relationship where someone is only with one person
  at a time.

- TRANSGENDER
  An umbrella term that encompasses people whose gender identity or
  gender roles differ from the ones associated with their assigned gender
  at birth. Not all transgender people choose to use hormone therapy
  or gender-affirming surgeries, and not all choose a new name or gender
  marker on their birth certificates and IDs.

2-Spirits

- TRANSMAN / TRANSWOMAN
  A man who was assigned female at birth / a woman who was assigned male at birth. Not all transmen/transwomen transition with the use of hormone therapies or gender-affirming surgeries, and not all of them change their birth name or gender identifier on birth certificates and IDs. Transmen and Transwomen can have any sexual orientation.

- TRANSVESTITE
  An outdated and problematic term because of the historical context of its being used as a diagnosis for medical and mental health disorders when referring to transgender or cross-dressing people. It was created to define transgender people, but it morphed into a slur. While it is no longer used in the medical or scientific communities, some transgender individuals are known to use the term as a way to reclaim it in a positive light.

- TWO-SPIRIT (OR TWO SPIRIT, TWOSPIRIT, 2-SPIRIT)
  A modern umbrella term used by some Indigenous people to describe gender-variant individuals within their communities. Not all Two-Spirit individuals identify with the LGBTQ+ community, and not all of them use "they/them" pronouns.

- XENOPHOBIA
  A dislike, hostility, hatred, or prejudice against people from other countries and also of that which is strange or foreign. This often has an overlap with racism based on an individual's personal prejudices.

FURTHER READING

The New York Historical Society wrote about an intersex person named Thomas(ine) Hall that belonged to a colonial Virginian community. Their story predates anyone mentioned in this book. [wams.nyhistory.org/early-encounters/english-colonies/thomas-ine-hall/]

One of the best-selling recording artists of all time, Whitney Houston, was in a queer relationship with her close friend, Robyn Crawford. This news came out after Whitney's death when Robyn published her memoir in 2019 titled *A Song for You: My Life with Whitney Houston*.

Harry Benjamin, MD, who had met Magnus Hirschfeld before and helped perform Christine Jorgensen's surgeries, wrote *The Transsexual Phenomenon*, an incredibly modern book for its time. It's well worth a read if you'd like to know more about the history of transgender people and would like to see how far we have come. Note: Harry Benjamin's book is not 100% up to date with our 21st century understanding of gender.

A close friend to Simon Nkoli and fellow GLOW member Bev Ditsie made a film about her relationship with him as well as their fight for LGBTQ+ equality in South Africa called *Simon and I* (2002). There are shots of Simon as a young activist as well as his later years when he was battling AIDS, all of which helped inform the imagery in his chapter of this book. You can host a screening of this film through the Women Make Movies website. [www.wmm.com/catalog/film/simon-i/]

The Library of Congress has set up a free Digital Transgender Archive to house thousands of digitized historical materials and other information on transgender history. [www.digitaltransgenderarchive.net]

Scenes from Magnus Hirschfeld and Richard Oswald's film, *Different from the Others / Anders als die Andern* (1919), can now be viewed online thanks to the UCLA Film & Television Archive—Outfest UCLA Legacy Project, which stands to archive and preserve queer and transgender films. [www.youtube.com/watch?v=-U_SJflgf34&app= desktop.]

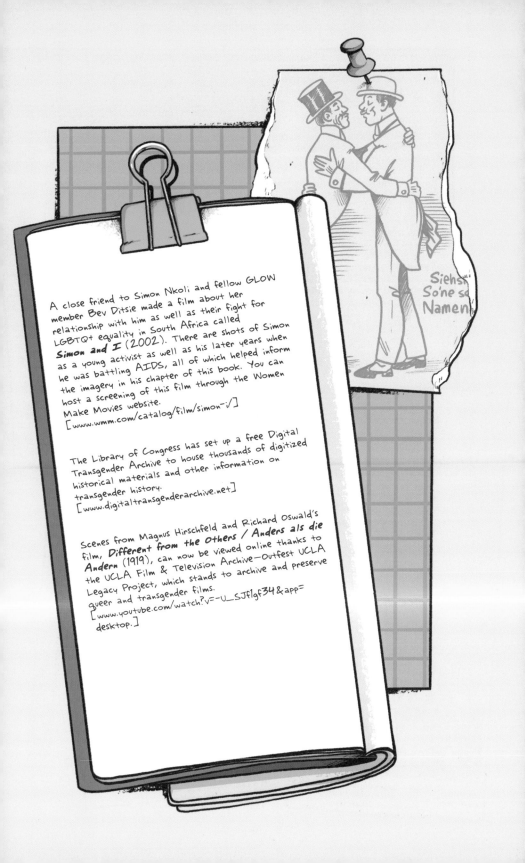

Siehst
So'ne sc
Namen

RESOURCES

Note: Most of these are American-based organizations.

TRANS LIFELINE –
   Trans-led organization that connects trans people to community, support, and
   resources to survive and thrive – 877-565-8860, translifeline.org

THE TREVOR PROJECT –
   The leading national organization providing crisis intervention and suicide prevention
   services to LGBTQ+ youth – 866-488-7386, thetrevorproject.org

CRISIS TEXT LINE –
   For anyone in any type of crisis. They offer 24/7 crisis counseling through text
   message – Text HOME to 747741, crisistextline.org

NATIONAL QUEER AND TRANS
THERAPISTS OF COLOR NETWORK –
   Aims to advocate healing justice by transforming mental health for
   queer and trans POC – nqttcn.com

COALITION TO STOP VIOLENCE AGAINST NATIVE WOMEN –
   Helping to stop violence against Native women and children by
                           advocating for social change – csvanw.org

NATIONAL SUICIDE PREVENTION HOTLINE -
Provides 24/7, free and confidential support for people in distress, prevention and crisis resources - 800-273-8255, suicidepreventionlifeline.org

DEQH LGBTQ HELPLINE FOR SOUTH ASIANS -
Confidential support for South Asian/Desi LGBTQ+ and Questioning Individuals, Families, and Friends - 908-367-3374, deqh.org

LATINX THERAPY -
Helping destigmatize mental health in the Latinx community - atinxtherapy.org

NATIVE YOUTH SEXUAL HEALTH NETWORK -
An organization by and for Indigenous youth that works across issues of sexual and reproductive health, rights and justice throughout the United States and Canada- nativeyouthsexualhealth.com

INTERACT ADVOCATES FOR INTERSEX YOUTH -
Uses innovative legal and other strategies to advocate for the human rights of children born with intersex traits - interactadvocates.org

BISEXUAL RESOURCE CENTER -
The oldest national bi organization in the U.S. that advocates for bisexual visibility and raises awareness - biresource.net

NATIONAL RESOURCE CENTER ON LGBT AGING -
First and only technical assistance resource center in America aimed at improving the quality of services and support for LGBTQ+ older adults - lgbtagingcenter.org

ANTI-VIOLENCE PROJECT -
Empowers LGBTQ+ and HIV-affected communities and allies to end all forms of violence through organizing and education, and supports survivors through counseling and advocacy - avp.org

ACKNOWLEDGEMENTS

I have officially crossed "get my first graphic novel published" off my bucket list, but I couldn't have done it alone.

First of all, thank you to my partner for putting up with me complaining about how hard it is to write a book and bringing me plenty of snacks during the process.

Thanks to my agent, Peter Ryan at Stimola Literary Studio, for believing in me and making this all happen! You've made the process of pitching books and creating stories so incredibly easy for me.

Thank you to my lovely editors, Liz Frances and Katie Fricas, for crafting this thing into not just a beautiful story about LGBTQ+ history and liberation but a memoir about living in the South as a genderqueer pansexual person. You both have pushed me and encouraged me to create something we can all be proud of.

Thank you to Will Roscoe the activist, scholar, and author for his expert advice on the story of We'Wha.

Thank ya to my friends and editors at *The Nib*, Matt Lubchanksy and Sarah Mirk, for taking on my stories about queer history. The comic about Magnus Hirschfeld I published with y'all allowed me to get an agent and pitch this book. I'm forever grateful!

And finally, to all of those who have been a part of me getting here: Ronnie Garcia, Steenz, Mark Bouchard, Hazel Newlevant, Archie Bongiovanni, Ashley Robin Franklin, Maia Kobabe, Jennifer Rapinchuk, Morgan Czeropski, those in my family that love and accept my partner and I, and all of the queer and trans friends in my life that have loved me, given me a safe space, and have listened to me. You are all beautiful and amazing people.

ABOUT THE AUTHOR

Shelby Criswell is a queer comics creator living in San Antonio, TX, using they/them pronouns. They studied studio arts at the Santa Fe Institute of Art and Design as well as illustration at Academy of Arts University. They have been creating comics and drawing since childhood. Shelby is an author of the *Terminal Punks* comic series and has had work in comic anthologies including *Sweaty Palms* and *Everything is Going Wrong*. They have also illustrated comics for *The Nib*.

Photo credit: Lumiere Tintype